A LITTLE BIT

OF

FAIRIES

A LITTLE BIT
OF
FAIRIES

AN INTRODUCTION TO
FAIRY MAGIC

ELAINE CLAYTON

STERLING ETHOS
New York

STERLING ETHOS
New York

An Imprint of Sterling Publishing
1166 Avenue of the Americas
New York, NY 10036

Interior text © 2018 Elaine Clayton
Cover © 2018 Sterling Publishing Co., Inc.

ISBN 978-1-4549-2872-0

Distributed in Canada by Sterling Publishing Co., Inc.
c/o Canadian Manda Group, 664 Annette Street
Toronto, Ontario, M6S 2C8, Canada
Distributed in the United Kingdom by GMC Distribution Services
Castle Place, 166 High Street, Lewes, East Sussex, BN7 1XU, England
Distributed in Australia by NewSouth Books
45 Beach Street, Coogee, NSW 2034, Australia

For information about custom editions, special sales, and premium and corporate purchases, please
contact Sterling Special Sales at 800-805-5489 or specialsales@sterlingpublishing.com.

Manufactured in Canada

2 4 6 8 10 9 7 5 3 1

sterlingpublishing.com

Interior design by Lorie Pagnozzi
Cover design by Elizabeth Mihaltse Lindy

Image Credits
Katja Gerasimova/Shutterstock.com
satit_srihin/Shutterstock.com (border)

CONTENTS

INTRODUCTION

Perhaps fairies and their ways have long been told of by quaint people in the days of old—or so it's thought to be. Many may have regarded such tales to be superstitious fancies, but to those who experience the phenomenon, fairies are very real and natural parts of our existence.

There is a heartfelt way of living that recognizes that everything and everyone is interconnected, therefore whatever occurs on any given day holds true meaning, whether symbolic or literal. This meaning is the profound sense that we are not alone in our struggle to survive. Nature and uncanny events are familiar and common, in fact. Living with a sense of innate oneness proves time and again that there are unseen helpers permeating our natural world, urging all of life to thrive.

And this is where a mysterious, mostly unseen fairy realm merges with our practical, physical world.

Though fairy stories have been passed down for centuries, such spiritual entities among us are experienced anew. Every person with an inclination to acquaint him or herself with wee folk find that those aren't just silly tales once told, they're accounts of ways in which spiritual beings reveal themselves to us.

And with general knowledge of the variety of fairies and their habits and traits comes the opportunity to claim them as one's own. This is so because fairies in our midst are as unique as we are, as individuals; there are no two exactly alike.

This book was written with the ardent wish for anyone who

has reflected upon, heard about, felt, dreamed of, or seen fairies (or for anyone who wishes to) to become personally able to commune with them.

As we delve into the spiritual essence infusing all growing life, we celebrate the benevolence and generosity of fairies whose radiance shines upon us; we comingle with nature for our very survival. Through tender saplings and spring-fed brooks, through noble trees and inscrutable mountains, fairies abound and reach for us to partake. They also caution us as we readily harm our environment without understanding we cannot be sustained without it. Fairies are among us, appealing to our love of life and our will to thrive, to strengthen the interconnectedness that makes existence possible. Where we meet them is in the deeply mysterious aspects of life through which fairies communicate and encourage us to abundantly prosper within our natural world. There they dwell, beckoning us. . . .

"COME AWAY, O HUMAN CHILD, TO THE WATERS, WET AND WILD . . ."

—W. B. YEATS

❖ 1 ❖

WHERE FAIRIES WANDER

How now, spirit? Whither wander you?
Over hill, over dale,
Thorough bush, thorough brier,
Over park, over pale,
Thorough flood, thorough fire;
I do wander everywhere.

—*A MIDSUMMER NIGHT'S DREAM,*
WILLIAM SHAKESPEARE

FAIRIES ARE KNOWN TO BE A "GOOD PEOPLE," a hidden and ethereal race of beings who appear as 3-D as any human or as hologram-like (colorful and mostly transparent) forms of all sizes. Luminous and airy, they may even appear quite fully human, although often smaller or in some subtle way a bit different than an average human (with very pointed elfin ears or large, mesmerizing eyes). Fairies are somewhere in a spiritual stratosphere between humans and angels, and by "somewhere" I mean we can't quite be certain as to "where" they are in relation to us. Yet just as you read in the poem on the previous page, they do "wander everywhere." We might sense them but not see them, or see them and question whether we actually did see them. They confound us!

Fairies are intelligent, blithe, and fluid entities of light and color. Since they can manifest presence of physical matter (appear to have a body) they are still able to flummox humans by disappearing at will. Folklore is rich in tales of such spirits among us. Theirs is a pure energy, infused in nature not limited to but often emphasized and expressed through growing plant life, infusing the elements and almost any aspect of our universe.

The path to knowledge of fairies is to approach all of nature with a deep sense of appreciation, gratitude with an affinity for the furtive, transcendental pulse of life permeating our natural world. It is to enter the dreamier, more mysterious aspects of who we are as living beings and what our universe is made of in its enigmatic greatness. Glimpsing into fairydom is to wish to perceive the fathoms of sea and sky; peer into the tiniest specks of pollen, pistons, and stamens; gaze upon the prismatic wings of the dragonfly; to consider the ways we humans are in awe of how all this life came to be.

MEDITATION: GET INTO A FAIRY REVERIE

Outside in the quiet of the day, whether you're in a city park or out in the wilderness, in a small garden or countryside, fairies abound.

In soft rays of sunlight illuminating tender tips of green leaves, a magical osmosis is underway. Verdant life spins life and the hum of bees among birdsong coalesces with the mysterious and ethereal. Humans are born of Earth and call it home, but it is also a place where fairies dwell, at the edge of our sense of time and space, of solid matter and light energy, in the mystifying forces of life as it continually expands. No wonder so many children recognize this otherness, this parallel fairy world when they're out playing; it is spellbinding and strange, yet it is ours; we grasp it and, alternatively, do not grasp it.

Children sense that life is not all as it seems on the surface, until we coax and condition them to more practical applications. They understand immediately and naturally that our propensity and habit of labeling and identifying nature is superficial and may not be the actual most important aspect of experiencing the world. They feel the exciting air of enchantment, of unseen fairy folk. They may shout gleefully at bubbly sea foam tickling their toes, knowing each drop of mist is a kiss from the Fairy Queen of the Sea, and frolic with mermaids they sense are right there with them. Or they'll leap outside into a simple backyard with the undeniable, thrilling feeling that something amazing is about to happen, something magical. They are aligned completely with their imaginations, knowing it is very much a part of this great expansion of the life force and the pathway to the playscape of fairies. They know that there is a dream happening, and we are in it.

Go There

Step outside into the dream that we call "just an ordinary day," watch the arabesque of a silky petal, fluttering like a ballerina's skirt, and hear the soft whisper of the pines as you are beckoned to the threshold of enchanted terrain. You may only be thinking of internal woes or plans, or how good or bad the grass looks, or how many weeds need pulling, but you are in the presence of fairies and have entered their domain. You may sense this and fall silent unto yourself, looking around as if being observed somehow; a peculiar feeling may surround you. Open all your senses and allow yourself to sense the question lingering in the air. Breathing, feeling the way Wind Fairies play at mischief. Gathering bluster, tree branches sway; their leaves tremble as they quietly rustle or sensationally roar a fresh and hypnotic message to you—*through* you. Fairies of trees, wind, leaves, flowers, and branches are in your midst and in your hair! They're moving through you, playing with you, reveling in their mysteries ways, and you're invited to the celebration.

Being in and with nature nurtures us as we, too, are creatures of life meant to thrive. Simply being in and with this alchemistic, instinctive world might be enough if we did not sense the deeper mystery in it, opening us to the feeling of exciting potential and wonderment. The unanswered question we sense is the stirring of our innate curiosity and a longing within our soul. That part of who we are wishes to know how to intuit the spiritual messages of the wind and trees, the tiny grass blades and the leaves unfurling, reaching for sunlight. Isn't there something more we cannot quite grasp? Don't we want to envelop the meaning held within the darkened bark of trees? Don't we wish to come to know the lovely contours of richly green moss patches on rocks? In our curiosity, we see life burgeoning as we ourselves ought to. The fairies seem to hold life-sustaining energy that supports us as we live and breathe. Fairies are part of this continual unfolding of life in ways we know not, or rather, we realize there is much we do not truly understand, but we can feel it and sense it.

We want to have knowledge of our natural world, of the land, the stars, and the tides, but even more so, to revel in how it makes us feel as it powerfully draws us forth, to swim, to play, to immerse ourselves as we once did as children. We climb summits to feel a stronger, triumphant sense of self, and we explore caves to go deeper into what is not commonly known or experienced. Nature becomes symbolic of and entwined with our inner knowing and concept of who we are, and that inner knowing tells us the spirit of life is inherently one and the same as fairy life. It is mysterious and ethereal, like us, even more than we are physical.

The realm of fairies is open when we allow ourselves a more fluid sensibility and acceptance of it, simply being in and with nature, to allow love to freely flow to and from our hearts, overriding our impulse to mentally control, characterize, and classify everything. Inhabitants of our environment beyond our textbook labels will tell us who they are if we listen and watch with a hint of expectation. This is not a mental process so much as an intuitive opening through creative, imaginative interplay with nature. However, this is not to say that fairy ways are only whimsical or trifling.

Fairies are fun, yes, and jocular and frolicsome, yet in their way they are very serious, somber, and tempestuous. They're as changeable as the weather. Inwardly, we know we must respect nature and the power within it to aid us or destroy us. Fairies are one with this natural momentum of the elements as we watch it do what it does. Fairies are playful and high-spirited, but not to be disregarded. As has been passed down to us through time, we know not to tick them off, these fairy folk—there is mischief in them when we do. They are not just passive presences, they are a prevailing life-force energy that we cannot deny, and yet they're elusive. Being engendered into fairy wisdom takes a willingness to open and develop the inspired, visionary, artistic, and mystical mien of our human essence.

We need a little bit of daring and a lot of friskiness mixed with quiet awe to engage properly with fairies. Fairies are entities that baffle, confuse, delight, and even aggravate, agitate, and throw tantrums until they get their way. They are the energy of "the will to thrive," and that's spunky. Fairies are helping life prosper, by aligning with it to funnel beauty and longing and love into each living particle. Watch anything grow and you will recognize it; you'll see tenderness, innocence, and also a dauntless presence of flourishing zeal. All growing life knows no other than to strive to prosper. Fairies are made of this abundant spirit of life. Look at a leaf as the sun bathes it. The leaf is more than willing to receive all it needs and asks for nothing less. The sun gives all it has to boldly give. This same simple determination to blossom, bloom, and triumph is fairy essence.

For this boldness, fairies are often seen as demanding and spoiled, full of spite if less than desired is given. Fairies, in their machinations, want what they want. A fairy will demand whatever it may need to survive and anything else it wants is expected to be given (for optimal blossoming, and more)—or else!

FAIRIES BY DAY, FAIRIES BY NIGHT

Fairies are best seen, they say, at twilight, the time that is no longer day, but not yet night. Time itself with its mysteries of light and shadow, as it influences our earthly orientation, becomes a portal into otherworldly dimensions and affairs. Such arcane activities of fairies vary from day to night, with many accounts of fairy sightings describing the strangely haunting rituals performed in the dark of night, such as gathering in a ring and dancing, or the Queen of the Forest calling out all her court to entertain her, alongside animals and in the light of the beaming moon.

Fairies have been seen merrymaking in radiance under a star-dappled sky in a hazy moonbeam glow, or walking and dancing, wailing and shrieking across rocky coasts, moors, or plains, banging shutters and rattling window glass on dark and stormy nights. There are all kinds of fairies and they each have their ways, so exploring them is actually very exciting. But first, let's first determine how a fairy differs from other spiritual beings because they are unique and in a role somewhat different from angels.

❖ 2 ❖

FAIRIES AND ANGELS

O, speak again, bright angel, for thou art
As glorious to this night, being o'er my head,
As a wingèd messenger of heaven.
—*ROMEO AND JULIET*, WILLIAM SHAKESPEARE

HOW EXACTLY DO WE DISTINGUISH FAIRIES from angels? All of creation, every particle of matter, is impregnated with abundant spiritual endowment, and both angels and fairies are in cooperative roles to bring about the most potential with that irrepressible force of life. Fairies are the delicate link between earthly life (that which is physical matter) and spiritual life (that which is ethereal), and they are, to a degree, subject to the same laws of nature as are we humans, and they're fiercely protective of it. Yet fairies are spiritual beings, able to pass through one dimension into another. In other words, they can slip into human-like 3-D form and cultivate life that is in 3-D form, and then disappear into the purely spiritual dimension unbound by matter.

Angels, on the other hand, are not subject to our laws of nature and function as spiritual advocates arriving to help us cope with these terms of natural law such as gravity, growth, death, illness, and increments of time. Fairies are coping in their own way a bit differently from that of humans, and need our cooperation, as they require (for their own well-being) respect from us for the elements, seasons, the land we inhabit, and all aspects of Earth life. Angels may peer into our world, see into our life situations, and even appear as human or animal to aid us; however, they are not of our world. Fairies are bound to our world, yes, in some essential ways, though they experience it uniquely.

Our collective human relationship to the subject of fairies and angels differs from one culture to another, and has evolved over time. Folk-pagan belief in fairies thrived for centuries but gradually changed in the western hemisphere, especially after Judeo-Christian religious teachings became dominant. After all, a pervasive notion of fairies described an idea about their origins: Fairies fell somewhere in between hell, Earth, and heaven. The story is that when the Gates of Heaven opened, angels streamed into heaven, but then the gates closed before fairies could follow the angels inside. So, in this narrative, fairies didn't quite make it into heaven. With that, they've been viewed as something like a less-than-divine variety of angel. If fairies flitted invisible among us on Earth, we'd be cautioned that it's best not to fraternize with them as they aren't worthy of heaven, and may not help us get there one day.

TROUBLEMAKERS

Fairies could be blamed for menacing, confusing, or upsetting events, especially unexpected or unwanted occurrences. And they were the easy explanation for unpleasant experiences and events that took place such as illness, bad crops, or other misfortunes. If a baby got sick and seemed different, parents might well have assumed that fairies switched their own fairy baby with the human baby (such substitute fairy babies are known as "changelings"). Likewise, if something happened we might call "an act of God" such as a seemingly healthy tree suddenly crashing down, witnesses with shivers up their spines might exclaim that angry or mischievous fairies had caused it.

Interestingly, religious authorities, though invalidating fairies and warning against interactions with them, in doing so in some sense acknowledged their existence. Admonishing against anything out there that might be evil, fairies certainly qualified in the eyes of religious leaders. Some pagan practices based on folk wisdom meant to appease or block negative fairy power were still passed down through generations, though, so the desire to ward off the threatening fairies still had a voice, even if only a whimper.

It may well have been feared that since there were also angels lost from heaven, who rejected heaven and became therefore tempters who took up residence in hell, fairies might be more aligned with them than with the angels they tried to follow through the pearly gates. On the other hand, anyone pondering might consider that fairies, like heaven's angels, might be here to guide and protect us. Either way, fairies remained a sort of odd mystery, and for many, just part of the old superstitions and not anything "real." These diaphanous beings remain among us on Earth, permeating flora and fauna, wandering wherever they like, but behind a gossamer veil. Their existence is largely denied or ignored by the humans who could commune with them.

BE CAREFUL THERE....

Whether considered real or not, good or bad, fairies generally were thought to pose possible threats, and such caution comes perhaps for good reason as fairies vary from nice to not so nice, and look out for themselves (their natural disposition to unyieldingly thrive). Unless they just happen to be fond of you or have respect for you, or see that you benefit the environment, beware! They're watching us closely as we go pushing and shoving our way through our time on Earth, often creating havoc in our environment (*their* natural environment!) without a hint of awareness as to what we've done, stomping around careless of the damage we cause.

WHAT IF?

Fairies by nature are feisty creatures, though their true existence may be denied by many in our day and age, that old belief in them hangs on under the surface of the most practical among us. A collective and general fairy-renouncing exterior has beneath it a big what-if, as it is part of human nature, or even perhaps cell memory, to wonder about the ancient spirits our ancestors told of for many centuries.

And again, since some religious teaching warns that having a curiosity of fairies might compromise a soul, that alone seems to be an admission of their existence. There are strange things out there that you could invite in far too close, allowing them to attach to you. Fairies, it could be warned, especially the ones that are not benevolent, might not be a good idea. And even the good ones take your attention away from devotion to the established religion you may be affiliated with, so generally major religions have highly discouraged and warned against fascination with fairies, as it is a pagan belief. More and more, though, people are embracing a sense of oneness and wholeness that does not exclude fairies from the lexicon of spirit helpers, and the lines between fairies and angels blur.

Also hazy is the way prior belief in fairies influenced religion. Over time, invoking God directly (and possibly angels or saints from their place in heaven) through established religious practices became the rule over communication or cooperation with vivacious garden spirits who may well be treacherous. Yet, rituals to ward off these jaunty but ungovernable creatures of lore may be behind many religious practices, such as baptisms. Babies are not said to be baptized to keep fairies away, of course, but to sanctify them and protect them from anything that may be treacherous, of the devil, or destructive to the soul; to wash away "original sin," or the in-born condition humankind must contend with—survival and basic instincts, temptation, and death—this includes wild spirits from the mischievous ungodly fairy realm.

The innate fear and our instinct to protect our newly born as they grow through vulnerable infancy and early childhood is indeed very strong, and it has long been a part of the plan to keep our younglings safe. Throughout time fairies or some other unseen malicious forces were believed to prey on the innocent. Baptism soon after birth certifies that no other spirit but God's should come near the newborn and somewhat replaced age-old practices such as putting a piece of bread into the blanket of a baby before going outdoors with it, to ward off any mean little spirits out there that might harm the child or steal it, as fairies are said to have done.

Fear of the unseen powers that influence our circumstances is part of our shared human condition; we can't explain everything all the time, and fairies have long been highly suspect! They have not really gone away or disappeared because of religious practices and beliefs. Most commonly, people give themselves the freedom to say their prayers the way they were taught, perhaps, but still put out some little gifts for the fairies on the night of the summer solstice, without feeling doomed or as though they have compromised their soul. And we love our fairy-tale, too.

Fairies get top billing in our contemporary life and have remained a much enjoyed subject in literature through folktales, fairy-tale, and myths, more as symbolic stories with moral lessons, with a modern sense that the fairies are make-believe. What was once open acknowledgment and concern about fairies and their antics has subsided in our time for the most part, except through our beloved stories.

There are many who have their own personal stories about fairies, though, and that magical place wherein they dwell, in between our experience of space and time, and an individual's fascination to rediscover them is keen. We, who ponder the existence of fairies seriously, alongside our love for angels, see the results of their manifestation, and know they work together for our world and individual prosperity.

❖ 3 ❖

FAIRY FOLK
AND
THEIR KIN

Down along the rocky shore
Some make their home,
They live on crispy pancakes
Of yellow tide-foam;
Some in the reeds
Of the black mountain lake,
With frogs for their watch-dogs,
All night awake.
—"THE FAIRIES," WILLIAM ALLINGHAM

THERE ARE MANY TYPES OF FAIRY FOLK THAT are commonly experienced and fun to learn about. Following are some you might like to get to know.

SWEET WILLIAM FAIRIES

A favorite of mine (formerly known as *Brownies*), these lovely, usually beautifully dark-skinned entities traditionally were thought to be benevolent in-house helpers. They were thought to occupy unused areas of the house and people kept a little stool or chair for them near the fireplace to welcome them. However, they also frolic in the garden, where they're often heard swishing through grasses.

Sweet William fairies play like mischievous, capering little boys and girls in the dirt and are boundless and rambunctious as they are little risk-takers. They befriend those who have compassion and who need a bit of playful rowdiness and daring spirit to break the monotony of their work day or to add excitement to their orderly days.

Sweet William fairies will watch all the goings-on from high branches or low greenery, crouching, smiling, and waiting to play with you or create a little mischief with animals and other fairies. Cats can see them and birds may chatter when they're nearby. In springtime and summertime, a Sweet William will sit savoring a honeysuckle flower inside a tent if you kindly create one for him or her. Their frolicsome cuteness is at its height by day, and at night, they are silent under the moon, sleeping in tree hollows, lush greenery, or secret areas in wooded places. For all their recklessness, they're actually quite affectionate and sentimental, and feel it most keenly at night. Outside you may hear one whimper in the dark, like a lonely animal, or you may hear things in the house moving or shifting—that would be Sweet William trying to help you out while you're asleep. And you may wake up to see a favor they've done for you in the house or outside. Traditionally, they were thought to fix or tidy up things for their human hosts, and this they'll sincerely try to do. Even if it doesn't quite go right, remember they mean well.

A friend who has a resident Sweet William fairy told of how in her storage closet she had an original piece of art, a painting of a landscape, placed securely above a cabinet, only to hear it come crashing down one night. The Sweet William must have liked it, she thought, and wanted her to have it out on display. He had climbed up to get a better look, and in trying to take it down from the cabinet, lost his little grip on it. My friend knew there was no way the painting could have just fallen from its secure place above the cabinet, and she understood the Sweet William, like a sweet child, simply wanted to have that painting to look at it. She had the frame fixed and keeps the painting out of storage and on the wall now, thanks to Sweet William!

In nature, these fairies prefer to inhabit areas with less horticultural fussing and are drawn to somewhat raggedy places that are overgrown, as they align with the energy of freedom, allowing plants to sprout a little wilder now and then as part of a necessary evolution in the growing cycles.

How Sweet William Fairies Help Us

Sweet William fairies will help in all kinds of ways, bringing a spirit of care along with a lighthearted joy into your environment. They play and appeal to your risk-taking and rather impulsive nature,

They encourage your spirit to "be you" and to branch out in life, without fear or too much self-criticism. If you need to give yourself more freedom to germinate your inner creative, adventurous ways, or if you've become bogged down in your routines in life, attract a Brownie in to your environment.

How to Attract Sweet William Fairies

Outside, let some areas be overgrown so a Sweet William can hide, leap, and frolic by day and sleep soundly nearby at night. Go outside and talk to every living thing out there and now and then leave a bit of sweet fruit under a tree for the Sweet William fairy. The idea is to create "party time" in the best way, making your garden or yard welcoming and relaxed. Inside, they want to feel at home with you, so bring in plants that have a playful energy about them and keep a window open letting in fresh air at times, even if just a tiny bit open. Get goofy and laugh. Let your Sweet William know you expect and appreciate all the kindness and help. Leave a bowl out and a little chair somewhere cozy for a Brownie to claim.

IMPS

Watch out for trouble! Imps seem to get into our most subtle energies of thought form and entangle it all up just for the fun of it. We have to watch what we give our slightest attention to as far as attachments or self-importance, because imps will play with that. For an example, let's say you have a favorite shirt that you just admired yourself wearing when posing in front of the mirror, or you fuss over the precious sheen on your new car. Next thing you know, the perfect shirt has a large coffee stain on it because the cat leapt just as you took your first morning sip of latte or when you get to the car it has a glaring scratch all the way down the length of it. *Ha-ha!* You can hear the imp laugh.

Imps feel our attachment energy to things and create challenges for us in the way of small interruptions, little screwups, and glitches. The positive side of this is that we get the opportunity to re-center our true priorities or practice grace through irritations in daily responsibilities. It helps to have a sense of humor. Next time you find your blissfully shiny car scratched in the most obvious way, take a deep breath and think of the ways in which even something like that just may, with a good attitude, align you with the best life can offer (such as when you take the car to have it detailed, you just so happen to be introduced to the romantic crush of your life while waiting for assistance).

Because Imps love to take your favorite things and mess them up, I do not even want to give them much space here in this book, lest I tempt them. Their humor is a little bit wicked and spiteful, yet they don't really mean much harm. Traditionally, Imps could be depicted perhaps more maliciously oriented, even looking like little devils, but were still also seen as mostly just pranksters, meddlers, and interrupters. They might lead someone down the wrong road or cause a person's sense of timing to have a comically (or unhappy) domino effect.

How Imps Help Us

The best way to handle Impishness in your midst is to be as centered and calm as possible, keep that sense of mirth in you, and be conscious of what you're attached to emotionally. Be ready to laugh and hold your temper—a flare-up of heated anger might only fuel the naughty Imp nearest you! Imps help us realign with our sense of decency and respect for others, our environment, and ourselves.

How to Attract Imps

Imps are looking for suckers all the time; you may be more interested in not attracting them. A great way to rally them around you is by your doing things that undercut or harm others in small ways or large. Imps are hungry for disrespect, teasing, cheating, and lying. They love that kind of mayhem, and if your ways have been less than honorable, it is possible things will go wrong from the moment you wake up until the moment you go to bed. The elevator will close on your skirt or the blender will go on before you've got the lid on tight. You name it in the way of unpleasant interruptions and chaotic scenarios, but Imps are thrilled to whip up mini disasters or tumult with long-lasting effects. The upside is to remember that even if you're encountering Imps while being the best person you know to be, they challenge all of us at times and serve as little testers to our sense of honor for life and for others. If an Imp causes disarray for you, let it serve as an opportunity to assess your integrity and respond with as much grace as possible.

CHANGELINGS

Some conventional and long-told fairy ways are disturbing, and I find the idea of changelings absolutely repelling. As we shall see in Chapter 5, which is about Irish folklore, fairies are thought to have a desire to steal children. When a fairy steals a human child and replaces it with a fairy spirit baby, the fairy baby is called a *changeling*. The human spirit of the baby is then among fairies and benefits them in various ways. In some cases, the fairy child's spirit, embodying the human baby, would get coddled and adored by the human parents. Therefore, the fairy parents hoped that their fairy baby would have a wonderful upbringing by its new human parents. Beauty in a baby or child increased the chances of attracting the covetous nature of the jealous fairies. Pampering and adorning a child too much also highlighted the child's attractiveness to fairies.

Another idea of changelings may have developed long ago as an explanation for upsetting conditions such as childhood sickness or disease. In these cases, parents of a perfectly happy, healthy child may have deemed that the child wasn't "being him/herself" after perhaps suffering maladies or permanent afflictions. The effects were as if the lovely, robust baby they once held had suddenly disappeared. Efforts were made to ward off this kind of fairy invasion and embodiment or switch of an innocent baby or child, and some stories describe ways in which the human baby's parents might get their baby back, involving serious negotiations with their local fairy rulers.

How Changelings Help Us

I think there is not much to be said about the idea of changelings as helpful, except to say the thought of them might remind us to take better care of our young, to focus on them without our egos attached, and to not be overly precious with them, using them for our own ornaments, or living through them by pressuring them to be reflections of our own vanity.

How to Attract Changelings

Ancient wisdom on this warned against too much coddling of a baby as it would catch the attention of fairies, rousing their jealousy. I suspect this was partly due to the notion that the more deeply you care, the more vulnerable you are if something goes wrong. This, combined with the thought that a child's ultimate survival meant they'd need to be stealthy, meant they had to be weaned with tough love, therefore disengaging from a baby's emotional responses was explained away as benefiting the baby in the long run. "If we don't pamper the baby too much, the baby will survive," i.e. not be stolen by fairies. Today, I'd say watching the infant very closely and protecting the baby fiercely, responding swiftly to its emotional and physical needs, is best for keeping away illness or disaster (components of the origin of the suggestion of changelings).

ELVES

An Elf is many things—hidden and playful, small and ethereal, or as real in appearance as any human, only much smaller. Childlike and friendly, they may be helpers with charms enough to aid someone in need, often doing so while the benefactor they help is sleeping. They are known to bite your toe while you're reclining, just to let you know of their comings and goings! You might recall stories such as a German tale, "The Elves and the Shoemaker," who were so kind to help the cobbler fix, polish, and craft shoes while the beleaguered cobbler slept, only to wake to find a gleaming shop with all the hard work done to perfection.

But Elves may also be full of spite and cause some irritation to humans, or even to seduce or trick them. Their nastiness may bounce back upon them and cause their plans to go wrong though. At their core they aren't meant to be irritable and mean, but more so fulfillers of wishes and makers of good magic and good deeds. They inhabit the rocks (as in Icelandic lore) and the woods, hiding and skipping along under peaceful trees, frolicking in the shadows or dappled sunlight.

How Elves Help Us

Elves may come indoors wherever there is a feeling of interest for them, or a perceived need for their assistance. If a home has birdcages in it, the Elf in your house may open the door and free the bird. Elfin schemes are usually for good, and they love the chatter and fun children have, so you are more bound to have Elves when children are at play in your home. And if anyone is sick in bed, Elves like to tend to their waning spirits and help them get better. Elves may also be found at the wayside for travelers, often at a crossroads, and disguised at times, too.

How to Attract Elves

When a human is kind to an Elf disguised as homeless or as a person who needs a helping hand, that Elf may reward the passerby for their kindness by guiding them well or leading them to some kind of good fortune. If the person is cruel to the Elf in disguise, they'll find that something will go wrong, as the Elf seeks to thwart cruelty in humans. And Elves of a similar cruel nature will be attracted to such uncaring humans. The best way to attract benevolent Elves is to be as kind as you can be with anyone you encounter. Elves are attracted to exciting terrain and can be found near ponds or brooks, in trees, near rocks, in mossy areas, and especially where mushrooms and toadstools grow. Tread softly while in Elf territory! You'll know you're in their sanctuary when you see toadstools, mushrooms, mossy patches, and clover or flowers, especially when growing in a circle. Whisper and sing sweetly knowing they hear you. Tie a cotton sheet or other large cloth to branches to make a canopy in the trees; Elves like it when we create outdoor environments for play and rest. Also allow anything flowering to remain until the buds fade, even weeds. Once they've flowered, you're safe to uproot them.

PIXIES

Sweetly attractive and spontaneous little ones are Pixies. They're very childlike in appearance with their large glossy reflective eyes, sprouting hair and small pointy ears, but they're not exactly guileless. Pixies can sense, see, and hear just about everything. Humans, with their emotional and mental energies and intentions, as well as thoughts (which we humans often think are secret thoughts known only to ourselves), are like broadcast news to Pixies—such thoughts rush through Pixies in the form of visions and instant knowing, as they are incredibly intuitive and able to "hear" us, even in our slightest thoughts. They are very sensitive and quick-witted.

Pixies love dancing and even a little bit of rough playing, flitting merrily among newly growing sprouts, as they love vegetation and encourage us to grow food, vegetables, fruits, and herbs. They are attracted to rich, wet soil and applaud us for watering our growing plants. They love chasing each other through thickets. When you hear twigs snap, if you look quickly, you may spot the flash of a Pixie as it leaps swiftly.

How Pixies Help Us

In all of fairy varieties, Pixies are probably the most comfortable and friendly with humans, appreciating any gifts in the way of clothing or food. They may, in a snit, pull clean clothes off the laundry line, topple baskets, or scatter objects around, but no real harm is intended and they're generally pleasant in mood and quite happy in temperament. They help us keep our patience when needed, and at other times encourage us to long for wholesome nutrition, nudging us to plant seeds, to rake, hoe, and water newly growing herbs and vegetables. They'll help you keep your garden well tended and will often appear as butterflies, so look closely—that may be a Pixie watching you fuss over your sweet peas.

How to Attract Pixies

Pixies love it most when you're keeping a kitchen garden filled with beans, peas, strawberries, carrots, and anything else edible. If you've ever tasted a bunch of grapes, a summer squash, or handful of berries with no flavor, this is because there was not enough Pixie influence in their development. Pixies are the great infusers of irresistible taste sensations and are needed to help edible plants hold zest and piquancy. They ask that you plant and grow with genuine love in your heart (they can feel this when it's present and when it's not) and ask that you do not cut back raspberry bushes that may spring up in unwanted places, at least until after they bear fruit. Pixies infuse flavors with their purest essence, which is that of the magic of delicious earth-grown food. Also, to appeal to Pixie magic, plant flowers that attract butterflies and hummingbirds, and use reflection pools or shiny spheres so they can look at themselves; Pixies love to primp a little. And Pixies are taken by small luxuries such as shiny ribbons or ornaments, when given as gifts. If you live out in a rural area, run free sometimes across an open expanse, or keep animals that frolic as Pixies love action and the thrill of dashing and leaping. Traditionally, out in open land, they are said to love horses, riding the wild unbroken colts across moors, hills, and dales.

DRYADS

Dryads are the indwelling spirits of trees and are able to slip out of their trunks and limbs at night, appearing as tall, tree-like white or gray shadows in the moonlight. They silently roam through homes, especially ones made of wood or old ones where rough wood was hewn for posts and beams. While inside a home, they may stand at the window, peering out at the moon-lit night, humming softly, getting a new perspective of their own wooded habitat from interior spaces. They are kind, gentle, and grandfatherly.

How Dryads Help Us

Dryads want to keep the trees they inhabit healthy and looking good and are sensitive to all the creatures that depend upon them remaining well-rooted and stable, so they need our conscientious care and appreciation of trees. They do not like when limbs fall from the trees they inhabit and prefer that their human counterparts collect any branches and twigs that may fall (it actually embarrasses them or makes them sad to have their own dead branches beneath their canopy). Dryads appeal to us to help them maintain the base of their trunks keeping it all tidy and delightful, and will acknowledge our care for them in return by keeping us safe as best they can. Dryads will not allow the tree they lodge in, or its heavy branches, to fall upon homes or people if they can help it. And they often convey mystical messages to anyone looking up at them or caring for them in appreciation. Messages such as "It is time for you to move on in life," or "Great change is coming." Conversely, they will deliver messages you may ask them to send out, to change the weather or to send thoughts or warnings to loved ones.

How to Attract Dryads

Clear any underbrush and broken twigs or limbs from any trees nearby. Inspect the tree for damage, look closely at the bark and even place a rock circle at the base surrounding the tree to let your residential Dryads know that you are focusing on them and wish them well. Be kind to animals that live in their branches and don't be too shy to talk, sit with, hug, or sing to trees that live among you. Try it and see what happens. These deeply compassionate, aged spirits are there to help us.

GNOMES

Gnomes are among the most known of fairy entities, as they have gained a cult following in recent times, seen as cute and jocular in popular culture. The frequent use of gnome garden statues has taken on new meaning, such as when someone did a stunt using a Gnome statue and it went viral online. A woman discovered her garden gnome statue missing, she assumed stolen, only to receive letters with photos of the Gnome statue in various locations around the world, eventually to be mysteriously returned to her front door again. Certainly, Gnomes are bringing out the creative and lighter-hearted sentiments and sense of playfulness in people (always a good thing!), but gnomes are actually heavy weights and not just the laughable tiny sillies in little droopy caps that they are perceived to be.

Gnomes are deeply earthy, and inhabit low levels under, especially mines or caves where raw garnet or other gemstones may be. They have a temper, can be fierce and irate, and should be approached with caution and sincerity. A Gnome may hide in a stick-covered fort under snow, built low into the ground near rocks and low-arching branches where you may see foggy plumes rising up with each exhalation on a frosty morning. You may mistake that for a warm spring letting off mist in the cold morning air. Or you may spot a gnome hanging upside down from branches on an autumn afternoon, doing exercises, or see a terse, chubby fellow rumble by out of the corner of your eye as he darts about gathering berries in summer. Gnomes raise their families and toil away, fretting about their concerns, hemming and hawing while they whittle and cook and do other chores. They make a type of ale out of brackish water and the juices of juniper berries and mint. At night, you may hear them as they saunter together arm-in-arm in the moonlight, singing drunkenly. At times you may hear screeches and low rumbles under your house or in the woods. This noise would be Gnomes arguing, fighting, or celebrating.

How Gnomes Help Us

Gnomes know their place and generally like to stay out of our way, and they do a good job of it. Our outdoor chores may have an impact on them, so stack logs carefully so they don't roll out dangerously when a Gnome sits on them, and don't damage large or small roots of trees. The root systems and underlying areas are the Gnomes' domain, and they will take care of this part of your property. They'll keep underground waterways unblocked and could divert water so it doesn't flood your home. They appreciate it when we don't move rocks around too much, as they may have their specific uses for them, such as for sitting, cutting up food, or hiding behind. If you do move them, ask politely! Gnomes will hear us if we are sad and try to cheer us up by making delightful blossoms appear, or by having a colorful feather float your way, or by asking birds to come sing for you.

How to Attract Gnomes

These private, often cantankerous entities are best settled nearby when we leave them be. Allow areas of dark underbrush near large rocks to remain a little private. Clear some, but not too much as these may be where Gnome families live, work, and play. Leave clear pathways for them, though, by placing foot stones from your home or patio leading to the garden or toward their little groves of trees or shrubs. They'll use them just as we do! And leaving a little sweetly scented tobacco out for them, or a pipe, might be nice now and then.

SYLPHS

There is an ungraspable sensual mystery and moonlight magnetism in the energy of the Sylph. The feeling of Sylph-ness is to have a fascination or infatuation with one who seems forever unattainable. A never-to-be-quenched desire comes with this elemental, because they are human-like but are truly creatures of air and therefore they're wisps of enticement, never to be pinned down. Deception and ruse is the language of this airy entity. You may feel a Sylph's presence by getting a kind of "champagne bubbles" feeling at your temples, or on your skin, with a tingling sensation down your neck or up along the insides of your arms. And then a sensation that someone of interest is thinking of you, though you may not even know who it is. When a Sylph is merging with you or whirling the air around you, a lighter yet sensual feeling comes over you. A quite sudden thought of positivity or ease may arrive out of the blue when a Sylph approaches. They range from kind to a little naughty.

How Sylphs Help Us

Sylphs can get you ready for love, for feeling sensual, and for arousing your interest and desires to mate. They whip around, invisible, making romance and love and seem not only possible but inevitable.

How to Attract Sylphs

There is the feeling that one does not attract a Sylph so much as a Sylph decides to visit you. However, the more you breathe deeply, allowing the air to become your focus, you will see that, as we pretty much ignore the air around us, when we really think about it, feel it, and become aware of it, it becomes something quite powerful. Air is what gives us the breath of life and Sylph energy is that which wishes to lighten your burden, giving you a feeling of floating or flying. Being naked in the air is one way to really connect with Sylphs; you will feel a lovely tingling sensation on your skin. This is a sensual practice and in so doing, you'll feel tempted to fall in love. When you think about it, it is air (Sylph) that fans the flames of the hottest fire.

NYMPHS

If you want to be at your utmost desirable, Nymph vibes are there for you. Sultry, sensual, sexy, and most alluring are creatures known as Nymphs. They get our hearts quivering as they tease us with their mysterious charisma. Enchantment and starlight appeal is their essence. They're seen in quick flashes of light upon water, or heard at times as whispering or gentle rustling in the night, like pillow talk whispers. They're shimmery apparitions of lust and their giggles sound like one who has known desires fulfilled. They may inhabit land, forested areas, rivers, trees, and even more cultivated areas of orchards, loving to roam on high in the groves of fruit or nut trees. Their loveliness gives wisteria and lilac their beguiling aroma.

How Nymphs Help Us

Similar to Mermaids, Sirens, and Selkies, these nature spirits express a sexual fecundity that permeates matter. They are shy but curious, playful and uninhibited in their seductive temptation and will charm you into your best, most captivating self. Fruitful, young, budding, and irresistible, they appeal to the passion within those they encounter. Humans may find themselves as if in a dream or with ravenous appetite for pleasure when Nymphs are near. Sitting quietly in the shade of a tree near a gentle spring, that sense of yearning and longing for love and fervor for life may peak within when a Nymph sets her gaze upon you. Nymphs want you to fall in love and have love.

How to Attract Nymphs

When you have a keen desire to be loved and to love another, Nymphs will draw near. If you wander through a wood or nearby a spring or brook, singing softly about love, Nymphs will hear you and follow. Where there is desire for love and ample sexual tension, a Nymph is not far off. See and especially touch everything outside, the leaves (are they glossy or velvety?), the flowers (are they satiny or plush?), and close your eyes as you feel the contour of rocks and the limbs of trees. Everything is sexually charged in a Nymph's world, and reacquainting yourself with textures is primary to stimulate your carnal nature. Nymphs wake you up to love making, and generously tantalize your basic sense of pleasure.

SELKIES

Have you ever gone swimming in the sea and noticed a seal playfully watching you from rocks beyond? That seal was probably a Selkie. They are sleek and buoyant, curious and flirtatious in a humorous way, but they could be somewhat sultry and lovely enough to capture the heart of their beholder. Old legends told of Selkies being vulnerable to humans who fall for them readily, and wish to make them their own.

How Selkies Help Us

Selkies remind us to be playful, to remain childlike, and to have lighthearted, lively thoughts. They're curious and comical; they help us keep a sense of humor about ourselves. Yet, like Mermaids, they, too, can be so curious about life out of water that they have been quite easily coaxed out onto dry land, where they shed their skin to assume human appearance. The Irish *merrow*, or *mermaid*, version of Selkie was said to have a cap that, once stolen and hidden away, could keep it land-locked for all its days, never to return to the sea again, its natural ebullient mood gone. In other tales, it was the entire skin of the Selkie that was shed and stolen.

How to Attract Selkies

Seeing a Selkie is a charming experience, but it is most likely you will not be able to get too close to one! If you have a cheerful, frisky feeling about you, watch for seals to come swim close by, and know that this is a Selkie in disguise.

ROCK PEOPLE

These invisible helpers, once called *Little People* by Native Americans, inhabit rocky cliffs near the sea and low-lying brambles and unkempt areas under bridges, in quieter, naturally wild areas. Truly they may be anywhere, in the tall grass of the high plains or the jagged buttes. They are near water such as brooks and rivers, bays and open shorelines, especially along the cliffs. They are in forests and everglades.

How Rock People Help Us

Rock People are the variety of fairies that are similar to Elves, but they're more private and have a solid sense of goodness and can be helpful in dire circumstances within their settings. Native American wisdom includes the Rock People as a race of beings quite fierce and frightening, however. If they see you harm someone or do something unfair, they may descend upon you. They can cause cars to stall or hide the keys so someone can't drive (in a case where they may be harmed or harm another).

How to Attract Rock People

They're all around, but when you need them and pray for help, they'll arrive and do just that. They'll move rocks or change the weather quickly, or persuade someone traveling to change the way they do things (by going faster, slowing down, or turning toward where help is needed). The Rock People are the best helpers when they feel they and the land where they dwell are respected.

MORE FAIRY FOLK AND THEIR KIN

Up the airy mountain,
Down the rushy glen,
We daren't go a-hunting,
for fear of little men;
Wee folk, good folk,
Trooping all together;
Green jacket, red cap,
And a white owl's feather!

—"THE FAIRIES," WILLIAM ALLINGHAM

THE BASIC ELEMENTS EACH HAVE THEIR OWN fairy folk. The seasons bring about changes in the natural world, and each one also has specific fairy folk. Read on to learn more about seasonal, elemental, and other fairy variations.

ELEMENTAL FAIRIES

The four basic elements are Earth, Wind, Water, and Fire, and they each have different attributes and personalities. So, too, do the fairies associated with each element differ in vast and small ways.

Earth Fairies

Remember playing in the mud as kids, maybe making mud pies or getting covered in it, and feeling happy to squish it between your fingers and toes? Fairies of the Earth are at work underfoot; they're the entities that govern the turn of the soil, helping the insects and worms that keep soil aerated and healthy. They encourage seeds, helping them germinate, and then coax the roots, urging them to have bold confidence to claim the soil for themselves. Earth Fairies are stocky with dark green, clay red, or brown hues. They have wings that resemble beetles' shiny wings. They're dense in appearance rather than holographic. They'll brush against your ankles as you walk, playfully tugging at you through the mud or pricking your bare feet with tiny sticks or thorns, just out of rambunctiousness. They are seen best in the gloaming light at end of day, as they like to catch a glimpse of the residential Fairy Queen who passes by in twilight.

HOW EARTH FAIRIES HELP US

Earth Fairies know that we come from dust and shall return to it, and that all living things on Earth eventually break down into the soil, in one form or another. While we are alive, the Fairies of the Earth long to claim us as the Earth's gravity and magnetic pull show us that our place is naturally the ground we walk on. They help us understand intrinsically that we thrive from the root up, and need a foundational base in which to grow truly strong. The electrons and healthy bacteria emitted through the earth have great health benefits to us, shifting our moods and regulating bodily organs. Children instinctively run outside barefoot, and adults should, too! Earth Fairies want us to be and feel grounded, to receive the gifts from the core of the Earth into our own core, and their mission is to give us reason to stabilize our lives through real depth; they want us to take root and know we *belong*.

HOW TO CONNECT WITH EARTH FAIRIES

Go outside as often as you can and walk barefoot. Try to get your feet against the actual ground, and simply feel yourself there, your weight sinking in or being fully supported by it. Earth Fairies will be present as you are infused with pure energy in the form of electrons, receiving and connecting with the biological rhythms of your planet. And don't be shy about digging, tending to gardens, and reaching with bare hands into the earth. You may not be making mud pies or sand castles anymore, but there are great benefits of getting dirty and standing upon or getting into the rich soil.

Wind Fairies

Fairies of the Wind are unseen hosts of change, riding on currents of air. They appear for only a moment as light, billowy feathers, with whisking gossamer wings. They're very blithe. They're usually white, or a blue so light as to nearly appear white, yet are truly see-through and not ordinarily visible. They like to whisper in your ear, tickle your neck, or kiss you sweetly. These fairies ride upon the wind, which is the breath of life, the breath of the earth itself. Wind Fairies know that as individual humans, we take our first breath upon birth and our last breath upon death. The inhale and exhale of our breath stays with us all our lives, and the pattern of our breathing is supremely important. Wind Fairies respond to the air pressure, both low and high, that creates our atmospheric conditions. We are either soothed and lulled by gentle breezes or ravaged by raging winds. Fairies of the Wind restore the harmony of the universe, striving for optimal conditions as they know the air pressure and wind greatly impacts the Earth and our lives. Seriously violent winds destroy our homes and stifling lack of wind is suffocating. A moderate wind may fill our sails and make the tree leaves shimmer.

HOW WIND FAIRIES HELP US

Despite their invisibility, Fairies of the Wind are concerned because as they flow with the natural movement of air, they see how easily our lives alter according to the atmospheric pressure influencing wind. When we work with them directly, through sailing, raising a flag, capturing power through windmills, or playing with kites, Wind Fairies are ecstatic and fulfilled. And we benefit from wind by listening to it, too. Fairies of the Wind will put messages in their delivery. As they sweep in, watch as the trees bough and the waves get choppy. Listen to it whisper or roar. You can receive true fairy wisdom about your practical life by tuning in spiritually to the wind.

HOW TO CONNECT WITH WIND FAIRIES

Send a signal to the Fairies of the Wind by setting up some outdoor chimes so that you'll remember to tune in when the wind comes through. Anytime you hear the chimes, take a moment to acknowledge that a mighty wind is passing by. Watch the clouds as wind emboldens them or blows through them like cobwebs. To hear what the Wind Fairies have to say to you, you will want to give yourself time to let the breeze be on you, to sweep your hair and remove the veil that shrouds you, to give you the sight of spirit. Wind Fairies are determined to convince us of their wildly robust presence, knowing that invisibility does not equate with non-existence. In the same way, spiritual influences affect us, as do emotions and energies, though we do not see these powers, we see only the affects they have on us and objects. Breathe deeply through practices such as yoga and attune to the breath of life, the authority of the wind, moving through us and our planetary atmosphere.

Water Fairies

We humans are a high percentage of water, and Water Fairies are able to surround us while also working closely with our physical systems to heal us. They may enter all seven chakras to balance and swirl health into you when you're unwell. Water Fairies by nature see that we are not separate as our internal waterways and external oceans, rivers, and lakes are one with us. Water Fairies flow where and in the way water goes, in the depths of the oceans with their waves, using stratagems to help the climate as it transforms ocean waters into vapors and then into rain that showers upon us and our verdant planet.

Fairies of the Water are luminescent, often the color of sea foam or sea glass. They tingle like champagne bubbles or massage you like hefty ocean waves. They have wings that are the pure pearliness of water droplets, and wear a hat that is actually just that, a lovely water droplet. They otherwise adapt to the waters they guide, appearing brackish brown or turbulent gold, aqua blue or deep-lake green. They babble, or they may tussle with Fairies of the Wind and send tempests in the form of wild, wet gales, ominous dark gray tornadoes, and hurricanes to remind us that nature's power is beyond us. Teaming with Wind Fairies is a dynamic way for Water Fairies to exercise wrath, which for us as humans has the ability to shatter illusions.

HOW WATER FAIRIES HELP US

Water Fairies want us to be in the flow of life. I once had a meditation at a time when I felt stuck. I saw a brook as though I were hovering above it. I heard an inner voice teach me, saying "Don't be like the water. BE the water." I suddenly felt myself smoothly moving over rocks, through sticks and downstream, quickly. I felt the sensation of releasing all tension and resistance, and literally flowing along with the current, down to the sea. Fairies of the Water know that we need to keep a fluid sensibility to endure life, that our deep roots of established habits and attitudes need water wisdom and that to be aware of the tides of our attitudes is vital to the way our life functions and unfolds. You know how it feels to be flooded with joy, sorrow, or anticipation. Water Fairies offer an outpouring of love through fluidity and buoyancy of spirit. Sinking is to be sad, without hope. Water Fairies urge us instead to float and play with the stream of life. Struggling against currents and tides only exhausts us.

HOW TO CONNECT WITH WATER FAIRIES

Physically, water heals and restores us to who we naturally are as we are so much made of water, and Water Fairies can do their best by us if we take more in. Drinking lots of clean water is essential to healing the body and ridding it of toxins, allowing the lymphatic system to flow like a mighty river. Fairies of the Water draw us in to play, whether by dangling bare feet into a lake, floating a paper boat downstream, or diving into the salty waves of the ocean. Water Fairies create bubbly sea foam to tickle our feet and make us giggle, and swimming is an excellent way to connect with Water Fairy energy. The ability to float and feel free of heaviness gives much relief to our minds and bodies. Water Fairies truly bond with us when we care for the water of Earth, not polluting it or abusing it. Take frequent salt baths (unless you live near the sea and can go for frequent swims!) and allow Water Fairies to soothe and relax you.

Fire Fairies

Once early cave people understood fire, they began to ease up on the constant instinct of fight or flight, as animals would stay away from the flickering flames. Fire Fairies, entities connected to our sun, helped humans gather around the heat of the fire, where the humans began to bond, eyes flashing in the light. Evolution of humankind has Fire Fairies to thank for helping us learn to bond, to cherish one another, to talk and listen to one another, and to forge tools to help us live more comfortably. Fairies of Fire know that there is great risk and severe danger in fire, and have an interest only in helping the Earth renew itself once it has been scorched. They grieve the losses caused by fires, but know we cannot survive without it. In appearance, Fire Fairies are wisps of flashing light, sparks, and embers. They're bright yellow, orange, or red, sometimes even white hot in color. Their wings are tiny blazing flickers; their expressions are rarely anything but severe and serious. Often, they appear in the immensely thick smoke that arises out of fire and ashes, faces bearing heavy expressions and portentous, threatening, and haunting features. Fire Fairies want us to take them very, very seriously.

HOW FIRE FAIRIES HELP US

Fire Fairies are fierce, dangerous, and serious spiritual entities. Theirs is a quick and unyielding force that can cause much pain and suffering. Yet Fairies of Fire wish to coordinate their efforts to best benefit us, which means they work closely with Wind and Water Fairies. Energetically, Fire Fairies understand that we have ardent, passionate emotion and they work with us to moderate our primal survival instincts through our fear, anger, agony, and sentiment. They don't want us to get burned by our own excesses but are very dominant in igniting and arousing our interest and excitement and truly kindle our desires for the good. They know that we generate heat through reactions to life, be it embarrassment, ire, exasperation, or grief. Fire Fairies also know that the smoke billowing from fiery flames is intoxicating and so are our ideas or feelings at times. They work intimately with humans, especially those drawn to heroic roles such as firefighters.

HOW TO CONNECT WITH FIRE FAIRIES

In fall and winter, gathering with loved ones around a fire pit or fireplace is ideal. Fire Fairies help us engage with the spirit of life when we carefully light fires (in fireplaces, candles, fireworks, etc.) to enjoy the warm, mesmerizing sparks and flames as much as the safe camaraderie our ancient ancestors felt when gathered around a fire. Kindling lights in the home at the dinner table, for example, will give true spiritual warmth to interior spaces. Fire Fairies, with their mysterious flames, lend charm and delight, mixed with romance and reverence, to all gathered. This is so because we know that fire is not a power to be toyed with, and therefore intrinsically we are alert as well as mystified when in the presence of it. Also, looking up at the stars and taking in the fire of their flickering light allows Fire Fairies to suggest ways we can expand, by opening portals to far away galaxies and giving rise to meteoric, sensational actions. Another way to honor Fire Fairies is through paying close attention to supporting the local firefighters who risk their lives fighting flames that destroy lives and ways of life. Fire Fairies know that humans work with fire in many ways to connect and that the punishment for fires out of control is so severe; the bravery and courage it takes to fight such flames is heroic.

Flower Fairies

Fairies of the Flowers are filled with light and fluttering energy, their wings like silken petals, iridescent as a dragonfly's wings. In fact, you may think you saw a dragonfly when in actuality it was a Flower Fairy you saw. They're lovely, each to each, with satin and silky skirts, tiny seed-like ballet slippers, and greatly colored petal hats and collars. They're sensual yet modest, bold yet coy. Their allure is intoxicating. They are pure sexual, fruitful energy. They carry different traits, some receptive, others assertive and each conduct specific duties. Some are lovely, dainty fairies who are also shy and a bit sensitive, for all their pride and glorious beauty. They need adoration and respect or they feel faint and their mood wilts. They do everything they can to earn praise since they aim to do only one thing, and that is to give beauty to the world through their fecundity.

HOW FLOWER FAIRIES HELP US

Flower Fairies make it possible for humans to live through their focus on pollination and fruitful fulfillment of life giving life. They help nectar flow to attract and seduce bees to spread pollen. In our lives symbolically, they produce in us the desire to germinate ideas and see our own potential realized, to sweeten our judgment as they suggest we develop our own advantageous flowering through worthwhile pursuits. They remind us that we are benefactors to others, and bear plenteous gifts to share.

HOW TO CONNECT WITH FLOWER FAIRIES

If you want to feel sexy, align with Flower Fairies! Try looking at life in a daring new way, freeing yourself of the weight of worry and allowing others to breathe their own air, to do as they choose to do, to learn through life as they deem best for them. Flower Fairies focus on their own great beauty and pay less attention to other flowers, and this is what each flower you behold (by admiring them on the stem or picking and arranging them in your home) beckons you to do. Flower Fairies want you to connect with them and receive the deep gratitude and love of self that they embody. The best way is to bring flowers in and pay attention to them. Admire them profusely and dance around them. Put flowers at your bedside and on tables throughout the home. Let them know you understand their exquisiteness. This will enhance your alluring qualities, bringing out your natural refinement and grace.

FAIRIES OF LEAVES

In every tree, bush, or plant, there are a variety of fairies that take part in the life cycle of their growing charge, even weeds, which often have special medicinal qualities. See the roles each variety plays, season to season:

Spring Leaf Fairies

In the season of springtime, Spring Leaf Fairies sing a soft and gentle song to wake the dormant twigs and branches of trees, readying them for new growth. First, they ease the cold and brittle extremities of trees and entice new buds and stems to shoot into being. A silent celebration takes place as gradually new and delicate lush green leaves begin to unfurl. Spring Leaf Fairies get the party started, creating an atmosphere and aura of teasing limelight. Spring Leaf Fairies chase away darker, colder days of winter. They're a bright, lucid yellow or green tone, very delicate and precious in appearance. They wear small incandescent caps, shaped like new leaves, jaunty, at a tilt. They wear tiny leaf slippers and their faces capture the look of serenity and expectation, with quick, green eyes. The moment they see you coming, they curl up into themselves on a twig, looking to all the world like a leaf yet to unfold.

Get ready for the spotlight, because Spring Leaf Fairies want you front and center! They'll illuminate you from inside out, excitedly making of you a "new leaf," tender and verdant, full of bright promise.

HOW TO CONNECT WITH SPRING LEAF FAIRIES

Spring Leaf Fairies stream their energy through you the same as they do through trees, urging the cells of the tree to start growing. They surge light through each cell of your being, and want for you all things new and exciting. With Spring Leaf Fairies, a human version of photosynthesis is underway when a strong, healthy person breathes life into her surroundings. This is what Spring Leaf Fairies most wish, that trees, bushes, and people harness energy for optimal transmutation. Inspect the small leaves that are beginning to grow on limbs of trees; lean over bushes that survived winter and talk to them as you'd want someone to encourage you. Relish in the newness by setting the stage for what is happening, arranging rocks under trees and around shrubs. Sit out among the trees as they begin anew, and hear the birds as they welcome and applaud them, knowing they inspire and remind you that you are always changing, and why not for the better?

Summer Leaf Fairies

Once the leaves and flowers have triumphantly celebrated and are fully blossomed, displaying their confidence, beauty, and will to thrive, Summer Leaf Fairies orchestrate tranquil dreamtime. Their energy is calming, quieting, and easy-going, as if to say "Let's just be still now and see what happens," after all that serious springtime push for burgeoning new life. Summer Leaf Fairies inspire idle, peaceful repose, for this is when dreams are stirred into being whether in morning, afternoon, or evening, mystical somnolence allows for conjuring the possible. Often in a heat haze, Summer Leaf Fairies will show you the shimmering love that surrounds trees. Gaze upon far-off trees as they sway in the breeze, because this is where wonderful ideas in the form of daydreams are given to our planet. These glistening, glimmering fairies are full of the sun's kisses as they look like a flash of light, passing by in the blink of an eye. You'll likely not see one, but more so be cajoled by one as you'll feel a sneeze coming on or get a little giddy, or even a little sleepy. They'll lull you into otherworldly realms of thought and ideas, these whimsical, chimerical Summer Leaf Fairies.

HOW SUMMER LEAF FAIRIES HELP US

Summer Leaf Fairies are here to bring peace to Earth through quiescence, each leaf touched by sunlight and shade in just such a way as to communicate well-being through acceptance of what is, yet with sincerest support for wish fulfillment.

HOW TO CONNECT WITH SUMMER LEAF FAIRIES

Take a nap under a tree, and picnic with leafy trees creating a lovely canopy for you. Gaze at sun-filled trees in the distance and let them deliver to you a wondrous daydream. Summer Leaf Fairies know that life, when given, seeks and desires love and experience. In the hush of a hot summer's day, new thoughts and ideas radiate through leaves, reaching out to you to accept life, make peace with it, and ready yourself to emerge with the ability to create new dreams come true for yourself and others. Sing to leaves as you walk by; the Summer Leaf Fairies will love it. Sing your own song, and tell them out loud (even if in a whisper) exactly what you'd like your life to be, and they will send this dream through each leaf, out to the warmth of the summer day and into the universe where dreams come true.

Autumn Leaf Fairies

After Spring Leaf Fairies and Summer Leaf Fairies have infused leaves with good, green, new life followed by hazy dreamtime essence, Autumn Leaf Fairies enter regally to signal that inevitable change is in the air. This change, though it means having to grieve for days and ways gone by, is utterly thrilling. Autumn Leaf Fairies hasten death of fully realized leaves, so that all future experiences waiting to come into being are prepared. First, Autumn Leaf Fairies begin with the oldest trees. These elder trees know the routine, and respond quickly. Sage, wise trees resign themselves to change, their leaves assuming autumnal colors as they allow their leaves to make an example to all others. They turn brilliant fiery in golds and reds. Autumn Leaf Fairies wear robes of the same flashing, impressive colors. They keep their heads held high and faces somewhat solemn. They spin and flutter, often falling from the branches along with leaves as they dance their way down to the ground. It is hard to tell an Autumn Leaf Fairy from one of the leaves it infuses, so alike are they in their spinning, twisting movements. Autumn Leaf Fairies infiltrate tree leaves and light them up in yellow, as bright magical lanterns along the roadways. There is a stunning majesty as Autumn Leaf Fairies command us to witness their yearly ritual. Autumn Leaf Fairies make dying look good. The dying of what once was reminds us that we are part of a life cycle, and evolution is our purpose. The ritual Autumn Leaf Fairies practice is a noble one to observe and honor.

HOW AUTUMN LEAF FAIRIES HELP US

Change is not comfortable, but is inevitable. Autumn Leaf Fairies wrestle us out of summer slumber and into the activation of those dreams we conjured while in our glorious peace of warmth and sunshine. As the weather cools, Autumn Leaf Fairies bring the sun's warmth through vibrant color in unbelievable beauty. Autumn Leaf Fairies understand their role is to help us transition, to chill us a bit into a resilient stance of readiness. They prepare us for another winter up ahead, knowing that they're paramount in giving us strength to transition. They take the edge off of it by astounding us in regal splendor. As we accept change, we simultaneously say farewell to what we've known.

HOW TO CONNECT WITH AUTUMN LEAF FAIRIES

If you can, rake up a pile of leaves and bring them into the house and roll around on them. Why not? Toss them like confetti and give jubilation for all you've experienced up to this point in life. Collect these vividly colored leaves as pages from your own diary or each as poems in their own right. Pretend each leaf represents something you learned or experienced. Glue leaves to blank paper and write under them what they stand for, or how they inspire you. Take photos of them in their gushingly brilliant hues, to share with others, kick them as you walk along. Breathe in the scent of cooler air. You will sense and recognize a melancholia associated with saying good-bye to Summer Leaf Fairies, but feel the intensely electrifying essence of Autumn Leaf Fairies who do create decay with as much aplomb as they are able. Witness the trees as they bear the loss of robed refinement, standing naked in the cold. So, too, do we humans at times have to face diminishing losses, but Autumn Leaf Fairies show us we can endure.

Winter Leaf Fairies

Winter Leaf Fairies commandeer the breaking down of dead leaves into mulch and mold. The bountiful harvest of fallen leaves is a boon to the grass and soil as they fertilize it and nurture it. Many wild creatures such as turtles use fallen leaves to nest and hide in. Winter Leaf Fairies try to persuade us to allow nature to heal the Earth through its natural process in the cycle of life. Our terrain and overall ecosystem requires this nurturing to be healthy. Winter Leaf Fairies lay low, are dark brown, and have deep golden hues. They're quiet and unassuming. They have leaf-shaped wings and mossy toned skin, yet can also be frost-colored white and blue over golden brown, their dresses quite like sheer layers of ice over darker fragmented shades of forest green. Most do not glisten in sunlight, but rather blend into darkness of winter understories, with just a fleck or two of diamond ice sparkle that may catch your eye. They rest on patches of moss and cover themselves with dry, moist, and dead, brown leaves. If you hear a rustling while out walking, look quickly, you may spy one!

HOW WINTER LEAF FAIRIES HELP US

As these fairies hunker down, they seem to be entities that have given up and welcome dying. The truth is, they're aware that through dying there is life to come, and if they can enrich the soil with their perished counterparts, they will present the environment with greater, far more vibrant life in springtime. They seek no attention, but savor the leaves we allow to stay and break down for and with them.

HOW TO CONNECT WITH WINTER LEAF FAIRIES

These cold fairies are best left alone; however, they give us permission to be left alone for a time, while we take the memories of the warmer days into our hearts and hibernate our resources to build up abundant strength for days ahead. Try sitting out on the rocks in winter and take in the scent of buried leaves as they steam up and protectively blanket the ground. Absorbing the energy of smoldering Winter Leaf Fairies will give you much strength and sustain you in your shivering dark months of reflection, allowing you to mourn the past without regret. What was is now passed, what is to come is not yet here, and Winter Leaf Fairies do not so much want you to linger in misery or sorrow as to slowly assemble and develop inner fortitude.

CRYSTAL FAIRIES

Don't suppose that cold stone you stepped on is not blessed with a fairy of its own. Crystals reside deep in many gray, unnoticed rocks that we dismiss as not too important. Often, great geodes are bristling pure light energy within their unremarkable gray outer layer. Crystal Fairies don't mind; they'd rather blend in. They consider themselves keepers of the bones of the Earth, and know that without them, our bedrock foundations would erode and our soil would slip, slide, and sink. Crystal Fairies clean the energy for all other fairies and life surrounding any area, be it forest, garden, city park, or rocky edged highways. They purify the energy by vibrating to the magnetic pulses of the Earth, each one connecting to the others in underground ley lines of healing resonance. Crystal Fairies may at times resemble the outer layers of a stone, being rounded or jagged, gray and solid, with moss cloaks and heavy, dull expressions in their eyes, so much to evade your attention. Their wings in such cases are granite gray with dollops of white quartz. Other times, Crystal Fairies bound about in full regalia, in amber or amethyst sparkles, wings of quartz, and headdresses of geometrically fantastic agate or polished garnet, for example.

How Crystal Fairies Help Us

Crystals energize us, clearing the emotional center of the body. They'll feel your emotions when you are near and will try to help you be aware of your own sensations from head to toe, to know where you are holding emotional frequencies. If your throat hurts, perhaps there is something you want to say that you feel you have not said? Crystal Fairies will sense it and try to heal you. Or perhaps you may feel heaviness in your heart; they will try to undo some of the tightness there. They literally will enter you to clear and cleanse you. Their ambition is to see you thrive with nothing blocking your good feelings from infusing you from head to toe. They see humans as a type of crystal, a conduit of electricity and emotional fluidity. When something blocks that flow, these fairies attend to that and bring the energy flow back. They do this for the Earth as well. If they're in rocks around your home, they are renewing energy and revitalizing the area.

How to Connect with Crystal Fairies

To feel the great benefits of Crystal Fairies, try holding several different kinds of crystals one at a time and close your eyes. Take your time. As you hold each crystal, you're bound to feel a difference not just in weight or texture but in energetic vibrancy. You might like to go to a shop where you can experiment and take a few crystals of your choice home. You can meditate with them and place them on different emotional centers of the body. Be playful with them and use them in your rooms to clear the energy. Place them in the sunlight to enjoy their magical appearance. The Crystal Fairies love to infuse us and our surroundings with their vivacity and sparkle.

DAWN FAIRIES

These are the fairies that call the morning, welcoming it into being. They sing the most soothing, momentous, and beautiful song; if you wake up anytime between about 3:00 a.m. and 6:00 a.m., you may hear it. Dawn Fairies are filled with grace and gratitude. They change in color as the light changes from deep, dark blue to egg shell white, with shades of pink and gold so as to blend in with the first blush of daybreak. They are peacefully powerful and harmonious fairies.

How Dawn Fairies Help Us

Dawn Fairies help us by instilling us with optimism as each new day is given in the energy of love. Their gentle presence allows us to quietly feel thankful for a new chance to interact on the physical plane, to learn and grow in consciousness as humans. With silent, pearlescent wings, they gather in chorus, touching our foreheads as we sleep and kissing each leaf, petal, and stone as they sweep through in flight as the sun rises. They rouse the birds from their nests.

How to Connect with Dawn Fairies

The Fairies of Dawn are evident to us when we feel a deep sense of serenity, and are relaxed knowing all is well. If you do wake up in the wee hours, stay calm and don't rush out of the sleep state by sitting up and turning the light on, instead, hover on the plateau of dreamtime and you may be able to hear them sing an enchanting and beckoning song. Dawn Fairies exist in the realm of pure light, love, and new beginnings, and bless each moment as darkness fades into luminosity. Your appreciation for a new day aligns you with their tranquil essence.

TWILIGHT FAIRIES

After a full day, ordinary daytime slips into an otherworldly realm of twilight; this is the most mystical hour. Here in this time and space where it is no longer day but not yet night, Twilight Fairies dance, play flutes, and bless the oncoming night. Eventide approaches, and Twilight Fairies, though not rambunctious or loud, are excited to accept the decline of the sun-filled day because the night is given to mysteries and dreams. The Fairy Queen is sure to emerge to witness Twilight Fairies caper in their starry robes and moonbeam caps of creamy glowing white.

How Twilight Fairies Help Us

These sweet, playfully curious and furtive fairies want to draw us out of routines, lighten our beleaguered woes, and cool us in the soft shadows of our innate goodness. Twilight Fairies want us to draw near one another, to whisper kind thoughts and keep a sense of mirth, no matter what the day had brought. Fairies of Twilight surround us with excitement mixed with holiness as we give over to the moon rising.

How to Connect with Twilight Fairies

If you'd like to blend with the Fairies of Twilight, know that they invite you to their celebration. Drawing near to this magical space and time, it is best to go outside and watch the light as it changes, to see the sun go down and notice the way the trees, leaves, grass, and water transform in a wonderfully, almost eerie way. Invite friends and family over and set up a twilight dinner table outside (in warmer weather) using only candles for lighting and you'll experience the enchanting sweetness of Twilight Fairies, as all of you sense the intimate thrill of the waning day, marveling at the approach of night.

FAIRIES OF LIGHT

Fairies of Light, also called Prism Fairies, belong to the color spectrum and are present in the reflections of emitting light that we perceive as primary (red, yellow, blue) or secondary (orange, purple, green). Within each hue, tone, and tint is healing power, and Fairies of Light are there to allow color to influence us for our well-being.

Red Fairies

Red Fairies are bold, passionate, and decisive. When we perceive the color red, the energies that emit from it are striking to us, causing our primal instincts to flare up. Fairies of the Color Red love to witness our emotional responses, centered on love, desire, anger, or fear. They wish to remind us that we have what it takes to survive and to feel life to the fullest. They're exciting fairies, confident and daring. They like us to be fearless, though, helping us to ultimately face our fears and courageously overcome them. They wear scarlet layers of chiffon dresses, robes, and swaths of wispy cloth. They have dark eyebrows and undaunted eyes.

Red Fairies help us reclaim our natural assertion and will to survive. They spark the heroic in each of us, and give us the knowledge that we have an intrepid spirit within, which we need to get through some stages of life. If things are dull and tiring, Red Fairies want to bump us into audacious, adventurous ways, smashing the porcelain preciousness that keeps us at times from true love, passion, and success. In your own life, Fairies of the Color Red want you to be noticed and to send signals to others that you are to be taken seriously.

HOW TO CONNECT WITH RED FAIRIES

If you sense that you are allowing weakness or a broken spirit to seep into your moods negatively affecting your life, get a dose of the color red! It may be a piece of furniture or you might paint an entire wall, but get some red going. You may also buy a red article of clothing or even lipstick. You might buy red shoes. Or simply get red crayons, markers, and paint and get creative with red for a while. Let these gallant Fairies of the Color Red remind you through the color red, that you have what it takes to survive and thrive.

Blue Fairies

Blue Fairies are as open as the sky and as wide as the ocean. They encourage us to expand our sense of ourselves and our world and love to get us out and about. As light emits the frequency of the color blue, the energy is cool and open, happy and new. Blue Fairies want us to keep it simple, to not complicate everything with overthinking and drama, although there can be a sadness described as "blue." This is because the deeper shades of blue appeal to our sense of duty and order, and when life events or relationships don't seem to be the way we ordered it up, we feel the sorrow in that.

HOW BLUE FAIRIES HELP US

Blue Fairies fly in with great expectations for us. They leap and skip, wearing pieces of sky—feathery cloaks of pale pastel blue to rich cobalt, and flit about with a strong sense of purpose blended with joy. They wake us up and get us moving. They playfully urge us to try new things, to laugh, to reach out for others in friendship.

Blue Fairies have a deep wish to expand our horizons. They know that without an open vista, we hyper focus on details or worry about the past, and the small issues that really should not take over our lives. Fairies of the Color Blue are here to cool our engines and prep us for smoother sailing waters, suggesting to us a happier and simpler outlook. Blue Fairies don't ignore our pain, but they will not rest until we transform pain into clarity, alleviation, and bliss.

HOW TO CONNECT WITH BLUE FAIRIES

Since so much of what Blue Fairies want us to do in the way of seizing opportunity, sitting down with a big handful of blue play dough is wonderful to try. That way, molding and forming shapes and rolling out chunky, formidable blue dough, Blue Fairies know we transform.

They want us to have a strong willingness to create and to experience life on our own optimistic terms. Otherwise, wearing blue is a great mood changer for the better, or tie-dying using indigo, getting those blue suede shoes and sitting in blue chairs. Or try connecting to Blue Fairies by watching or floating in water that is swimming-pool blue or the sea in all its varying shades of blue and even singing the blues if you can't get beyond sadness. It will help you release tension and allow for Blue Fairies to swipe the slate clean, to usher in for you all new blue-sky days ahead.

Yellow Fairies

Yellow Fairies are sensitive, as the color yellow emits a glow of sweetness, innocence, and youth. Yellow Fairies tend to be shy and small, but energy moves through them quickly, like lightning. They will spark your senses and zing you with a zesty little shock. You'll know this has happened when suddenly you become aware of something that you had not realized before. You may not know where it comes from, but you will not be able to deny the information. Yellow Fairies, for all their grace, activate stunning, flashing knowing and prod us to be conductors of this high vibration. They are tiny, and wear high, yellow-toned garments. As they zip around, they look like fast flashes of light on water. They have a temper, but it is quickly gone and would like us to know a forbearance of sensitivity is at times best when sprinkled with a dash of verve.

HOW YELLOW FAIRIES HELP US

Yellow Fairies, like the color itself, touch us deeply, calling out our inner child and humorously befuddling the overly serious in us and among us. A Yellow Fairy might kick a mean teacher in the shin (she won't know what that sharp, little pain was!) and will urge you to defend the ones who cannot defend themselves. They're quirky and nice, and they also want to help us develop sunny graciousness and to welcome others with a kind heart. They'll tip you off as to what and who to avoid. Ignore them at your peril as they mean it when they convey to you information that you need to know. It will arrive in a quick flash of thought or image in your mind. For all that spunky alertness though they aim to soothe, brighten, and give solace to others as well.

HOW TO CONNECT WITH YELLOW FAIRIES

The best way to benefit from the color yellow and their governing fairies is to allow a buttery beam of sunlight on your back each day, or to sit in the sunshine for some amount of time every day. Feel the color yellow on your skin as it revitalizes you. Using yellow in your surroundings also helps. Try doing an entire table setting in all yellow; yellow plates, napkins, flowers, and even some yellow food. Yellow Fairies want to jazz us up into doing things differently, to be unique and fun. Wear a yellow scarf or get a yellow pillowcase. Eat butterscotch. It's all good with some yellow vibration around you, and know that they want you to be you—uniquely yourself.

❖ 5 ❖

STOLEN BY FAIRIES

Come away, O human child!
To the waters and the wild
With a faery, hand in hand,
For the world's more full of weeping
than you can understand.
—"THE STOLEN CHILD," W. B. YEATS

WILLIAM BUTLER YEATS AUTHORED deeply inspiring books on Irish folklore, preserving and sharing unique and fantastic stories, which were for centuries part of the Celtic oral tradition, giving us precious and compelling access to the fairies of Ireland. Among those stories is the concept of the "stolen child," the one perhaps taken by fairies or the one drawn forever into the midst of magical fairylands. Yeats's written retelling of ancient tales takes us into wondrous realms within the freshly dewy lands where children frolic upon emerald sun-warmed hills, fairy rings, and mystical waterways of Eire, and allows us to take adventures there as well. Yeats invites us "with a faery, hand in hand" into the unknown, where we spin and whirl ourselves into supernatural terrain, perhaps never to return. His writing brilliantly captures our voracious yearning for the incorporeal, the breathless ambition to go beyond our heavy woes of this world, escaping into the trance of fairylands unknown. Yeats brings us to the muddy and marshy edge of the earthy and boggy world as we know it and guides us as we fall into the alluring, ethereal habitat of the fey and delightfully peculiar.

I am certain Yeats was himself a fairy, perhaps stolen by humans because it is said that he pined for the supernatural all his days.

HOW FAIRIES CAME ABOUT

The Irish Celts lay claim to fairies more than any other culture, and for excellent reasons. I recall going to Ireland and while visiting the grave of William Butler Yeats, author of literary treasures including "The Lake Isle of Innisfree," a poem about children being stolen by fairies. While there, an Irishman told me his version of the well-known story of how the notion of fairies began in Ireland. He said that there was a great war, the Battle of Benbulben in County Sligo. And at this battle, the Celts were fighting a powerful people known as Tuatha Da Danaan, and the Celts were defeating them. When the Irish won, those they defeated said, "You didn't defeat or kill us, we simply became *invisible*!" And so from that point on, those vanquished in the battle transformed into powerful incorporeal beings, undefeated. They became fairies. At the site of that battle, they are said to come and go through a door on the side of the mountain Benbulben. From that time on, they are known to have existed (and still do live) in the fairy rings or mounds and cairns found all over Ireland.

There are a variety of Celtic fairies, including Leprechauns, Banshees, Elves, Giants, and Brownies. Celts, from ancient Druid days through to our contemporary times, have told stories of personal experiences of encounters with fairies, yet the fairies are not secluded in Ireland or Scotland, Wales or England. They can be experienced anywhere, but I will say that if you have an inclination to learn about fairies, Ireland is a great place to begin your venture.

In Ireland during at outing with tea and scones, I watched as adults with their toddlers and young children ventured into a forest on the site of a former estate. The mothers and fathers sat on logs and talked. As the children played, the parents discreetly placed coins on mossy patches of rocks and fallen branches, without the children seeing them do it. When the children found the coins, they happily proclaimed the fairies had given them the money. What I loved about observing this was the adults' desire to culti-vate and nurture a sense of the magic and the notion of fairies with their young ones. Fairies in Ireland are a very real aspect of Celtic identity and upbringing.

Since elves and fairies do "wander everywhere," as Shakespeare wrote, stories of them are told just about anywhere.

Here is an account of a leprechaun sighting as told by Sandra Martin in her book *Snapshots: Memories and Recipes*:

In addition to cultivating the vegetable patch, I also worked in my flower garden at which was about a mile from the Dairy Barn, up a dirt road.

Right by my home driveway was a barren, rain washed hill without much vegetation. I thought it needed some love or, at the very least, some improvement. I first dug a small garden near the walkway to the back door. I planted variegated green and blue-green hostas there because it was under the shade of several big oak trees. I dug a curvy furrow from the hosta bed down the hill about 20 feet. I walked around the farm fields and picked up rocks to build a little retaining wall. I knew that if I didn't build a retaining wall the rains would come and push my carefully dug up and composted beautiful, raw, virginal dirt right down the hill and into the lake. The rocks worked perfectly.

I planted lavender and pink Rose of Sharon along that wall as well as petunias, and whatever package of flower seeds I happened to see at the Dollar Store. I also planted purple foxglove in honor of my Dad who survived his heart disease so many years thanks to the digitalis derived from foxglove....

Each spring I dug out more of the hill and built more rock walls. I bought and planted hydrangeas, holly bushes and shrubs; so many shrubs that I've forgotten their names. I dug up starter plants from friends' yards, old plants like nandinas and the ubiquitous purple iris. At garden centers, I almost always purchased the dry, sad and barely-alive potted plants. The ones that looked like they were on their last legs were the ones with my name on them. I felt sorry for them in the nurseries.

The hill started to bloom and be a joyous, happy garden. It glowed. Lilac bushes near the walkway to the back door always smelled so heavenly in the summer. In every season, friends wanted to walk through my garden when they came to visit. Eventually, my nephew helped me to build a water garden and place heavy flat rocks around it. It was beautiful.

Often, when I was in my garden, which was a lot, when I wasn't traveling or working on the Dairy Barn, I wondered about fairy people, leprechauns, and elves. Were they real? I'd sing to them. I'd ask them to show themselves. I felt their energy. The garden was a magical place. I painted a big sign that I nailed to the garden shed: The Fairy Garden. But I saw no fairies.

After working in the garden I often went upstairs to sit and read. Or work on a proposal. Mental stimulation after all the physical work.

Visitors often commented that my house was a terrarium. I had trees I'd moved around for 20 years. I had a jade tree that was almost four feet tall, a gorgeous plant, and it was always in my bedroom in a place of honor, with perfect lighting, because it was a sensitive spirit. Naturally, I talked to all my plants because they were old friends.

On this particular day, I was hot and tired and I had a fan blowing on me while I was reading. I was sitting in my comfy chair by my jade tree happy as could be. Not thinking of anything special, not sleepy, nor anxious, just even-keeled, with a book in hand. I thought I saw movement out of the corner of my eye and turned to the jade plant. And there looking right at me was a leprechaun. He was right out of central casting. He was sitting easy as pie on a nice fat limb of the jade tree, one foot up, elbow on his knee and just smiling at me. Green clothes, cute face, smiling twinkly eyes and he looked at me as if to say, "Oh, so you can see me now?" I was amazed, awed and excited, all at once. I just stared. Not saying a word out loud but thanking him in my mind over and over for showing himself.

After a short while he just started to fade away until he had disappeared altogether. I smiled and gave a thankful prayer for that beautiful gift.

Following is my own personal recollection of an encounter with "wee folk" or Elves from an experience I had while across the sea from the Emerald Isle in Scotland. I call it "Scottish Rock Fairies Saved Me."

In Scotland, along the rocky coast of the Irish Sea on the Isle of Aran, I had been walking with my husband at the time. I had just had a baby and was still somewhat weak, but we decided to get fresh air and understood there was a pathway along the shore, then we'd go up a footpath to a farmer's sheep field, and then we'd walk along the road and end up at a pub, where we could rest by a warm fire. As we hiked along, over stepping stones and shells, we realized that we must have walked too far and missed the footpath up to the farmer's field. We also noticed that the tide was coming in and the sun was going down. We knew we would not be able to head back the way we came or we'd be swept into the cold sea in the darkness. We looked up and saw what seemed like an easy climb along a cliff with ferns and rocks; it looked inviting and not at all difficult.

However, as I climbed, I realized it was much more steep than I had realized, and there was an area that I could not summit. My feet were on a very small ledge, and the next ledge up was at my chest level. I did not have the muscle to hoist myself up—one slip and I'd be dead. I had turned my head slightly to see that, clear as ever, any bit of wavering imbalance would send me crashing to the rocks below. Carefully, I searched my footing with my feet; I slid them all around the small area where I stood to see if I could step on something that would lift me. In a quiet panic my feet carefully slid all over the small ledge but no luck—there was nothing to step on to help me! There was no rock there to step onto so I could get a bit higher and lift myself over onto the higher ledge at my chest level. I was doomed.

I felt a horror and urgency I had never felt before. It was a feeling of certain, real death if something didn't change. I shouted up to my partner who climbed ahead of me that I was stuck. I said the truest and deepest and most ardent prayer of my life. I asked for help, or I would die. I said I didn't want to die, as I had just given birth to a baby boy.

Praying, I suddenly felt an obstacle with my left foot, and lo and behold, there I felt a nice, large rock, round and smooth by the feel of it. With my left foot, unable to look down at it, I explored this stone—it was fixed, it was solid, it was large enough to use as a step up. But it had not been there before! I knew it wasn't there just moments ago because, believe me, I'd have felt it there. I carefully stepped up on it and very slowly got myself up onto the next ledge. I was still so alarmed, but once I made it to the next ledge and then to the few smaller bits left to climb, I collapsed exhausted onto the long, soft grass of the sheep field. I told my then-husband what had happened. I explained to him how, just now, at that very moment, I almost lost my life. I was never more upset but grateful to be alive. It took me a few minutes to just calm down from the ordeal. As we got up to walk to get to the farmhouse to borrow a phone and get a ride back to the house (we had no interest in the pub after that near catastrophe, and it was getting dark out) I walked beside my husband. Then I felt a light pressing and swooshing feeling down my back. I said, "Oh, my hat must have come off," assuming perhaps that brushing against my back was a hat sliding down. I turned to pick up my hat. Then I realized, *Wait a minute, there's no hat.* I had not worn a hat—it was not even wintertime. I instantly saw in my mind's eye that the swooshing feeling down my back were the caring hands of two wee folk who lived in the rocks, who supplied me with a solid, round rock to stand on to lift myself, to save my life. They were not too tall, were pudgy, and looked similar to the rocks in that area, with round features and stocky arms and legs. Their hair was dark and straight as sea grasses. I had a feeling in my heart that was one of deepest humility and love. My prayer had been answered and I felt God gave me the help through these two fairies of the rocks at the coast, along the cliffs of the Irish Sea.

I will never forget that feeling of searching desperately for a rock where there was none, and the amazement of finding one that suddenly appeared, and then the caressing brush of love on my back after I survived the ordeal. The Rock People in Scotland provided exactly what I needed at a dire moment.

❧ 6 ❧

ENTERING FAIRYLAND NOW

Come up here, O dusty feet!
Here is fairy bread to eat.
Here in my retiring room,
Children, you may dine

On the golden smell of broom
And the shade of pine;
And when you have eaten well,
Fairy stories hear and tell.

—"FAIRY BREAD," ROBERT LOUIS STEVENSON

WOULD YOU LIKE TO GO TO THE PLACE where fairies flourish? Hearing and telling of fairies is a time-honored way of traveling to that magical realm. Actually, you are there in the blink of an eye, always at least partly there because their realm is between "here," our physical world, and "there," our ethereal world. I say "our ethereal world" because we forget we are just as much made up of invisible spiritual, emotional, and mental energy as we are of material form. So it is easy for you to enter into fairy knowing because we are always at the threshold of awareness of it, if not somewhat at least conscious of it. The realm of fairies is ethereal and in between our day and night, within but also in between our leaves, branches, rocks, and dirt. They are not exactly in the foreground or the background. They are not only in space or negative space, but in between all spaces. We sense and feel them, and then again, we don't. Theirs is a mysterious domain to us, but not a far-off one.

HOW TO TRAVEL TO FAIRYLAND AND ATTRACT FAIRIES TO YOUR PLACE

The most immediate and essential way to attract fairies besides listening to and telling stories about them is to watch what children do and recapture for yourself the feelings of wonderment. This is required as it is your passport to fairy ways and knowledge. As a child, you may remember you once raced, unbridled, roaming and leaping among the wild reeds of sprites and pixies, sensing them there. But somewhere along the way you possibly lost that passport, or it was taken from you by strict border guards (parents, teachers— all meaning well but giving you other tasks, and places to go or to think about) and you never renewed it.

Children understand to their core that they can transport themselves at any time to fairyland. They know that the meaning of "real" is subjective and an open definition. If a child wants to play Cinderella, the living room becomes Cinderella's lonely kitchen or bejeweled ballroom. The chair becomes the gilded coach and an oversize shirt is suddenly a glamorous ball gown. And no amount of adult pessimism could take that "reality" away from the child who is engaged in this imaginative place conjured by willpower to pretend, without hesitating in the slightest.

Children, especially before the age of reason, less than seven years of age, generally spin energy full of their magical thinking as much as operating out of or within our practical, logical understanding of our surroundings. They are conditioned away from this immensely creative power and gradually, over the years, develop skills quite different from the ingenious expressive, intuitive parts of their intelligence. Watching young children at play outside, one can witness the direct connection they have to the grass, the trees, the wind, the plants, and sky. They play without the separateness to the land; they feel intrinsically connected with it. They splurge headfirst and barefoot to discover their surroundings, with the expectation of finding the answer to secrets held within their environment, exploring areas adults tend to think nothing of, climbing in trees, weaving clover necklaces, and watching clouds form into faces and animals. They may race around on anything with wheels to feel the wind in their hair and play with the feeling of flying, of balancing while in motion. This kind of spirited playfulness is not giving them access to fairyland as much as it is purely *of fairyland*. They're already there. They know it, too, and so do the fairies.

Many adults speak of their memories from childhood of rushing out of doors perhaps to the edge of the water, or ambling through greenery, forests, and dales, or even a small backyard, inwardly thrilled knowing there were fairies about. They recall the feeling of utter joy and inhibition, perhaps with the feeling that leprechaun gold might be found in the deep shade under umbrellas formed by tree branches and leaves, or other cherished fairy surprises waiting to be unearthed. Trees, flowers, rocks, birds, and animals held for them the sense of adventure, and hidden riddles waiting to be solved.

Adults rarely step outside with this kind of openness and spirit of adventure with the expectation of magic. We tend to stumble around, looking down, deeply in our moods. With appreciation on a good day, we may walk around outside with a tendency to examine and label everything, or with the frustration of all the things that must be done. Or we may even be power walking or jogging, just another thing that has to be done in a day, swiftly moving under arching trees more noble than any stage ever set upon which to live a blessed life, having no clue as to the wondrous surroundings we are supported by.

If we want to commune with fairies, it is very necessary to approach nature with the same exact thrill and mystification present in us as new, young people, before being conditioned away from our creative instincts, which were paved over by cemented layers of duties, finite practicalities, and stifling logic. We must open to our own inner mystical sensing and knowing and feel with our hearts the passion for life we once felt as children, and not be ruled by the goals and standards we have set for ourselves as though such goals is all there is to a life well lived.

Fairy energy is spiritual, it is innate natural energy, and it is vibrating life and creativity at each moment of the day. As our hearts beat and we breathe. We, too, are made of the same stuff, really, and that is the propensity to thrive and create. Fairy knowing is creative, life force energy.

Try these basic and simple practices to remember and easily enter your own portal to fairyland:

❀ Walk outside with the desire to feel the grass between your toes.

❀ Inwardly say hello to every bit of greenery you encounter, as well as rocks and birds.

❀ Take naps outside.

❀ Sit in the grass or under a tree and watch/observe without having to label everything.

❀ Breathe deeply and notice the way your skin and hair feels in the wind by closing your eyes.

❀ Gather rocks and arrange them somewhere outside where you can feel creative joy (under a tree or in a patch of moss).

❀ Lean on trees and feel the energy within them.

❀ Hug trees or sit quietly with them for awhile.

❀ Pick up fallen branches from under trees and gather them out of a feeling of care for them.

❀ If you are cultivating a garden, see the landscape as theirs more than yours, design it with the natural character in tact (don't push away hills and drastically change the fundamental structure without inwardly asking the fairies who reside there).

❀ Touch and nod to trees and bushes as you go by (who cares who thinks you're crazy?!).

❀ Create fun fairy forts. Be playful with rocks and branches.

❀ Take pots and fill them with soil and create a mini garden for fairies.

❀ Leave sculptures or statues outside to let fairies know you understand they may like them.

❀ Take photos of small moments outside—the wonder of a flower, a budding branch, or a leaf in autumn.

❀ Get closer to leaves and peer into flowers.

❀ Grow plants you've always loved, including vegetables.

❀ Sing to the sky, trees, animals, and birds.

❀ Listen more to the sounds of birds and the breeze in the trees.

KISSED BY FOREST FAIRIES

Try asking for a sign from the fairies. I did this recently, and then forgot about it. A day or two went by and I received a text from a friend. She said she had gone mushroom picking with a group of people and had sautéed some for me to eat. Her message said, "These mushrooms were kissed by Forest Fairies!" I took that as my sign!

By the way, joining a group of mushroom hunters and pickers might be a fun way to connect with fairy energy, or perhaps with a walking group, or just a friend or two who likes to imagine finding fairy magic right along with you.

ROCK IT

A playful sense of wonderment can also allow you to be fairy-like in giving out love and magic. My sister finds rocks that are painted with positive and loving messages. There are Facebook pages and other social media devoted to this activity, where people who find such painted stones can look at the messages and even try to track where the rocks end up, as they get picked up, enjoyed, and then put in new places for others to find. This is very much a way to connect to fairy energy and the mirth and feeling of expectancy in painting, then placing the stones as surprises others will find is so magical and whimsical. Not only that, but a simple, loving message found by someone having a hard time can give them the encouragement they need to find solutions to whatever hurts them or worries them.

Try using divining rods (otherwise known as dowsing rods) to determine where water is flowing below the surface on your land. This process is wonderful, because the rods also cross if you pass over a granite rock that may have a large crystal geode in it. We look at gray rocks and think little of them, but certainly many of them have gorgeous crystals within that we never knew were there. There is a great granite shelf running through the bottom of my house and crystals are bursting out of this rock. It is a white quartz crystal and makes me very happy to see. I started a rock garden all around it where it juts out to the side of the house, to celebrate its beauty.

YOU ARE
YOUR FAIRY'S
KEEPER

Moonbeam steps down the silken ladder
Woven by Mrs. Spider
To ask her to spin him a net
To catch the stars.

—"MOONBEAM," HILDA CONKLING

DO YOU KNOW YOU CAN CREATE YOUR OWN understanding of the elemental and ethereal in your midst? You as an individual may develop your understanding and knowledge of fairies unto yourself, unique from any other people's sense of knowing fairies. To do this though you have to want to connect spiritually with nature and spend time cultivating a relationship of self to spiritual presence. As mentioned in the previous chapter, this is where imagination is fundamental because opening to the seemingly impossible frees us from restriction and limitation. Being mirthful and expansive, joyous and curious is required!

I will share some of what has come to me in my explorations and visions of fairies and their comings and goings. And, likewise, you can write down anything you sense, feel, see, or dream in relation to fairies, and build your own theories and knowledge of fairy characters and fairy ways.

AUBREY, KING OF THE ELVES

Aubrey, king of the Elves, is a merry-maker and is chief musician. He was born singing and when human babies sing in their cribs, it is a sign that King Aubrey favors them and has given them the gift of music.

He strums softly by day or night, plucking reeds and vines, or drums furiously, thunderously, using stones, wood, and water. The bedrock trembles and echoes when his mood is angry, and honeysuckle's tiny petals trumpet sweetly when he is tenderly content. His piano keys are made of crystal and gem varieties, be they emerald, sapphire, or quartz of all kinds. You can hear his crystal chimes best at before dawn and at dawn (but not so much after), as you come awake from slumber.

If you place polished gem stones (semiprecious or quartz crystals) in a circle near the base of a tree, or in a special clearing you prepare, he may play music with these stones for you, but only if he chooses and only when he desires, so you'll have to remember to listen! If you believe you've heard a ballad played on the stones you left out for Aubrey (by getting a quiet feeling of being called forth while you hear faraway music), you may race to see if the gems you placed outside for him are still there. You will probably find they were slightly shifted. However, they may be put back exactly as you left them, by his courtiers.

He and his court love quarries and forests, where they dance and laugh or weep and moan lamentations, depending on the king's sentiments. A dark, somber mood may fill a glen, an open field, or water's edge, only to change quickly to a brighter, lighter aura, when King Aubrey's temperament changes from heavy and sad to joyous.

King Aubrey's melodic rhapsodies are so wondrously life enhancing, as he plays at night, he brings the seedlings into stem growth and buds into bloom. You will wake and see that some plants have grown much overnight, some appearing when they were not there the afternoon before, and others having budded or bloomed. His fertile and sensual presence makes him the most adored of all Elves. Flowers quiver and shimmer with love and anticipation when they see him. Trees nod and bough as he passes by. Crickets are his musical mates, and grasshoppers are his footmen. Frogs are his horses. The female Elves in his court weave clover crowns for him and velvety suits of plant fibers, as if made with the finest spun cotton or silk.

You may hear Aubrey, king of the Elves, play, sing, or laugh, for he frolics at night in celestial luminescence, at his whim, full of mirth and sometimes intoxicated by Elfin liquor, made from any combination of juices from plants, especially juniper. This favored drink is carefully fermented by day and night with mint added or essence of various flowers.

Though you may hear him play, thinking it the sound of the bullfrog or the night owl, or coyote in the distance, he will never perform on demand. He plays only as he desires, when and where. He is a perfectionist. His music is a pure expression of Elfin elation or sorrow and longing; his heart lovelorn or requited, he beautifies the surroundings through his song.

The queen bees are said to glow like luminous moons deep underground as his music plays. Cocoons twist and wrangle by his chorus as butterflies are coaxed out of their encasements by his adoring serenade. His orchestral sounds beguile all of nature toward thriving. Foxes laying low underbrush in dark of night peer out from under waxy leaves and gnarled twigs as they watch King Aubrey while he plays. While he fiddles, drums, or sings, birds sleep soundly, dreaming of walking upon the Earth while humans rest, dreaming of flying and soaring through timeless corridors in the astral realms. The songs of King Aubrey affect humans and animals alike, the resonance and rhythms ebbing and flowing, carrying us where we need to go, readying us for a new day. A mysterious, unspoken awareness comes to us from King Aubrey, and our own life essence and growth in waking days, as well as during sleep, is intensified.

If you wake at or around 3:00 a.m., it is quite possible the aria of fairies and elves, their rich chanting and chiming in time with King Aubrey, has awakened you from slumber.

King Aubrey is a natural prankster, jovial in his mischief. And he can leave a path of destruction behind him. You may find branches snapped or clay pots broken, fence gates awry or other things out of place or damaged if King Aubrey and his midnight revelers came through. The best way to respond is to sing in the garden, hum while doing work outside, and keep a gentle, quiet spirit while appreciating all elements growing around you.

SOLAH-BAH, FAIRY QUEEN OF MOSSY SHADOWS

In the area where I currently live, there is a fairy queen who has made the entire street so magical, everyone comments on it. Visitors to my house say things like, "I had no idea this street existed; it is magical!" or "This place is like a secret fairyland!" And they are right.

There are many, many fairy queens, each having her own territory, and as on a chessboard, they supremely rule—and one here in my area as there is also one in yours. They grace the environment where they reside. They hold court and decree, usually with kindness and patience. At times, they are cunning and clever. They will protect their domain with severity if need be.

In suburban areas where outlying enchanted fairy queen land has been violated, the queen will try to mend and fix and heal the land for the birds, plants, and animals. If humans use harmful chemicals, she will not be able to encourage spiritual thriving in that area. Tightly landscaped areas where humans have used pesticides and have changed the character of the land in drastic ways are void of magic. You can tell by looking at these overly manicured places; they're sterile and uninteresting, cold and impersonal.

In my area, Solah-Bah is a moss- and shade-loving queen. Let me tell you about her. She delights in children; wishes for rocks to be surrounded by grass varieties with small areas of lichen and moss; and creates canopies with lowered evergreen tree varieties, giving humans, especially children, umbrella shade and tent-like areas, which create secret hideaways to play in. She delights in the laughter and free-spirited capers of children, and loves it when they climb trees and skip through grassy, mossy areas. Birds gather for her, chattering, warbling, and tweeting. Even young ospreys fly overhead in honor of her. She is a benevolent and gracious fairy queen!

GET TO KNOW THE FAIRIES IN YOUR AREA

Take a blank notebook or sketchbook with you outside in your area and be ready to jot down what you see and hear, and what feelings you get from your environment. Even if you're in an urban area, find the places where trees grow and animals gather and sit quietly, writing what comes to you in the way of spiritual presences within the living plant life. As you continue this practice, opening your heart to your own creative and imaginative life force energy (that's fairy magic!) you will discover that there are particular fairies right there near you and with you. And then you can communicate with them, watch out for them, and share your fairy knowing and encounters with others.

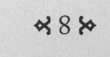

CHILDHOOD TRAVELS TO FAIRY LAND

There are fairies at the bottom of our garden!
It's not so very, very far away;
You pass the gardener's shed and you just keep straight ahead—
I do so hope they've really come to stay.
There's a little wood, with moss in it and beetles,
And a little stream that quietly runs through;
You wouldn't think they'd dare to come merrymaking there—
Well, they do.

—"THE FAIRIES," ROSE FYLEMAN

WHEN I WAS ABOUT FIVE, I WAS STAYING with a neighbor for the day, and my little friend Johnny's mother was taking care of me. It was summer. In fact, it was the summer solstice, and I heard of it for the first time that day. I was standing in the kitchen when Johnny's mother said, "Today is the day to leave gifts under the tree for the fairies."

Transfixed by this, I recall going outside and putting some little flowers and other items at the trunk base of the tree. Ever since that childhood summer day, I look for "fairy entrances" in trees, and I see how the combination of rocks and moss at and around tree trunks' base reveals genuine entrances (front and back doors!) for fairies.

Some fairy homes are massive and grand, with moss carpets and great granite steps. Others are modest and rather hidden, but look closely at the trees around you and see there is always some place where fairy folk come and go. Look up and down the tree to spot entrances at higher levels. Look all around the tree at anything growing or where rocks are placed. Also, if there are acorns with the tops off and you find those little tops—collect them, they're the hats that the fairies have lost while running to and fro. You may line them up somewhere or put them in a little bowl outside so the fairies can come and sort through them and reclaim them.

DONOVAN OF THE WILD FOREST

There was a little bridge near the school I attended when I was in first and second grade, and often, after school, I'd put down my satchel and saunter down the embankment to run and skip along on little islands where the stream flowed under the bridge. There were no trolls there, but there was a magical Elf and he gave me my own elfin name, and it was Donovan. I happily jumped through reeds and grasses as tall as I was, smelling the sweetness of the grass, picking buttercups that grew beside the water and taking a close look at spiders or bugs that I saw down there. Mostly, though, the high-spirited feeling I had there filled me with such energy. I leapt and skipped so much, I felt I was flying.

PINE TREE FAIRIES

At another point in time, a few years later, we had moved and I was no longer Donovan of the Wild Forest. I was unhappy at school and filled with upset feelings most every day after school. There was a pine tree behind my house that towered well over it. I let my hands get sticky, with the scent of turpentine, climbing up this tree every day after school. As I'd go higher, the branches became smaller and more flexible. At the top, or very near it, I stood, holding on to the branches and feeling myself, with the tree, as it gently swayed in the breeze. Gradually, I'd begin to feel better. The tree seemed to care about me. I had a feeling I was not alone. I remember climbing down once and slipping. I felt cradled as branches below me seemed to come together to make a basket for me to land in. I easily regained my grip and my feet found good, steady branches as I slowly climbed all the way down. I never saw the Pine Tree Fairy friends there, but I felt them, and I knew they were with me.

YOUR OWN CHILDHOOD FAIRY MEMORIES

Try meditating for a while on places where you once played and ways in which you felt or saw fairies in your midst as a child. As you delight in your own memories, write down and tell others of these unique and personal stories.

FAIRY WAYS: VISIONS AND DREAMING OF FAIRIES

I met a little Elf-man, once,
Down where the lilies blow.
I asked him why he was so small
And why he didn't grow.

He slightly frowned, and with his eye
He looked me through and through.
"I'm quite as big for me," said he,
"As you are big for you."

—"THE LITTLE ELF," JOHN KENDRICK BANGS

I T IS POSSIBLE WHEREVER PEOPLE LIVE, WORK, and prosper during their life span, a host of fairies live similarly, dwelling right there, in another dimension, invisible to us for the most part, within the same territory.

COWBOY PIONEER FAIRIES

My brother had a vision as a child in Texas that showed him an entire quaint little village of fairies who had small thatched houses, with rounded walls. He said they were an agrarian culture with farm animals and dressed like pioneers. He said he saw that the women wore long, sturdy skirts and long-sleeve shirts with aprons. The men wore hats and knee-length pants with vests and coats. Some smoked pipes, he said. They were an active and peace-loving people. He said they were musical and did ritual dancing. They were entirely human-looking but no taller than six inches. They lived in close quarters with their sheep, pigs, and cattle in corrals.

He saw this vision as it flashed in his mind's eye while at church one morning. In his vision, he saw them in their daily actions and was enchanted by them. When he came home after church, he quickly darted to the backyard to find them. He knew they were between the cherry trees and the fort my dad built for us that we called "the Clubhouse." He searched but only saw the typical dry, yellow grass of hot summer. He saw no fairies there in the area where they had been in his vision. But he felt and inwardly knew they were there.

STUDIO FAIRIES

Fairies are ethereal and communicate through dreams, giving humans ideas, advice, and warnings. I once dreamed a pleasant and sunny lady fairy told me to please put growing grass in my studio. In the dream, there was a tray of dirt and grass blades shooting up from it. The feeling she gave me was that it was fine to see the outer world from my large window near the drawing table, but I was to bring "a living thing" into the space as well. It was as if this would help bring spiritual benefit to me. Perhaps she was informing me that it is easier for fairies to help us inside our living and working spaces if only we allow plants to live there with us. I have noticed, too, that plants that are happiest are growing strong when the energy of the person who cares for them is positive. At the hair salon I go to for haircuts, the owner's orchid is humongous! Compared to other orchids, it is outstanding in size. And the salon owner told me that she knows it is a "she" fairy that dwells within this orchid. Since the owner is always cheerful and loving toward others, and has placed the orchid next to her and at a large window, the orchid flourishes like no other!

NOMA WEDDING FAIRIES

There is a type of fairy I was told about and shown in a dream called Noma Fairies. They are like the nomadic travelers of the fairy kingdom. In the dream, I saw a small group of silent fairies gathered in a hallway. All wore white, all were women. I carefully studied their features, which were somewhat delicate. They appeared very human, but there were differences that gave them away. One feature difference was that bridge of their noses was flat if it existed at all, so they had almost, but not quite, a concave appearance in the middle of their faces. And their ears were pointed, but mostly hidden beneath soft, silky light-brown hair. I saw that they were not smiling, but rather had a kind of serene melancholy about them. It was their presence altogether though that gave them a unique quality—a silence and a gentleness.

I was told in the dream there was to be a wedding and that is why the fairies were gathered. At one point others came out into this hall, one carrying a baby that she carefully placed under a bench to keep from being trod upon. The baby had a bright, almost orange glow and was not at all upset about being placed under the bench, and was smiling broadly.

FAIRY OF THE TURTLE EGGS

Another fairy dream someone had who recounted it for me, was set at her rural property. What she saw in the dream was an area where she knew in waking life turtles laid their eggs, so she had always kept that area covered with rocks so the eggs could not be mowed over or stepped on. The fairy in her dream was like my Noma wedding band of fairies, very much human-like in size and demeanor with the exception of her great wings that hovered over the eggs. This fairy was carefully extracting the turtle eggs out of the ground, using a straw. In the dream, the fairy looked directly at my friend. My friend woke up with a strong, peculiar feeling, but did not fully understand why the fairy was doing what she was doing. Is it possible this fairy protects turtle eggs and moved some from one place to another, and appeared in the dream as a way of saying "thank you" to my friend for her conscientious attention to the area there where turtle eggs are laid and hatched?

LOOK
FOR THE
GREEN MAN

Every fairy child may keep
Two ponies and ten sheep;
All have houses, each his own,
Built of brick or granite stone;
They live on cherries, they run wild—
I'd love to be a Fairy's child.
—"I'D LOVE TO BE A FAIRY'S CHILD,"
ROBERT GRAVES

HAVE YOU EVER LOOKED UP OVER THE RIM OF your teacup and seen a bearded green man look back at you? The Green Man is the term to describe fairy faces that appear in tree leaves and boughs and woodland logs or branches. Often there are several in one clump of trees, and each face has its own personality and expression of mood, often perhaps masculine or feminine but just as often androgynous and serious in appearance.

ROCK FACES AND ROCK ELVES

You may see faces in rocks, as do the people of Iceland who have the "hidden people" or Elves in the rocks, visible all over Iceland. When I was there, I felt I was on the surface of the moon, it was so unusual. So many volcanic rocks formed great mounds and seemed to be covered in a white kind of fur or plant, like sugar-coated nuts. And then there were large, jagged rock faces on the sides of mountains in the near and far distance that clearly held facial features and expressions.

You do not have to be in Iceland to see the fairies that inhabit rocks. I have seen faces of warrior chiefs on the red Rocky Mountains in New Mexico, too. Are there rock faces in your area? It is wonderful to go out on an excursion to find them. They often find you, as in you suddenly realize you see a face in the rock staring at you, but sometimes we need to go about our daily business, inclusive of the intention to see fairies.

In my neighborhood, I was just on a walk with my dog on our quiet street (which everyone says is magical and must have Elves and fairies living in the trees and rocks) when I saw a large rock with several shards of rock under it that had broken off and were so shiny they looked like slices of silver. I arranged them on clear soil so they could be seen as a footpath for wee people (fairies and Elves, Gnomes and Pixies, etc.) and so that perhaps the children will notice how lovely this silvery rock is. Part of me believes the fairies of the silver rock chipped away those silvery bits themselves for the children to see because just yesterday a few delightful children were sitting on that rock singing into their iPhone, making a little music video. There is Elf magic in the form of rocks and trees right in that little area where the children activated such happiness. And just a few feet away is the most spectacularly grand evergreen tree that has a hideaway under it where the branches sweep and fan out down to the ground, like a big hoop skirt, and you can go inside that pine needle hoop skirt and be encircled by the branches and slightly obscured by the pine needles, with enough room for many to play and sit. A large, unusual toad stool grows there also—more evidence of fairies!

Lucky Rocks and Geode Surprises

Rock Fairies are full of personality, and you can see it in each rock you encounter. If you really want to have fun, buy some geode stones and crack them open with a hammer (generally you place the stones in a sock before hammering so the pieces don't hurt you). I recently bought five such stones and was excited to crack them open. Each had some kind of crystal inside, except one; that rock was empty and hollow inside— such is the pursuit of crystals. But of the ones that did have a crystal, I placed the shimmering pieces with potted plants, where they look so good. Generally, it is believed that we should not move rocks, and certainly should not collect and take them out of their natural habitat, although we often do. You'll know when it is okay to take a rock and keep it because you'll sense whether it seems right. Rock Fairies love for us to value them and want us to benefit from the resonance therein.

Look for faces in all the trees, rocks, shrubs, and logs—even in the sky. You'll sense a blessing as well as a quality of love and a seriousness about them. And let them know you know.

ANIMAL AND FAIRY COEXISTENCE

A fairy went a-marketing—
She bought a winter gown
All stitched about with gossamer
And lined with thistledown.
She wore it all the afternoon
With prancing and delight,
Then gave it to a little frog
To keep him warm at night.

—"A FAIRY WENT A-MARKETING,"
ROSE FYLEMAN

ANIMALS AND BIRDS HAVE LONG BEEN known to carry messages for fairies. People have recognized the way animals aid us in countless ways, either in terms of knowing what needs to be known or through protection of one kind or another.

There is a natural way in which the animal kingdom species alert one another of approaching danger. In South Africa on a safari, I witnessed the way this alarm system works. I believe it was birds making a frightened sound and then the monkeys heard and started chattering and then the zebras heard the monkeys and started running around and before you knew it, a lion was approaching. From one animal species to another, their response to imminent threat was like a shared warning system for animals to know something that might eat them was coming.

So it is natural for animals to signal one another, and us, and we should be aware of what they're doing, for our own good. Other than that, we may see that animals offer another kind of very important gift, and that is much in the way of spiritual communication.

ANIMAL MEDICINE

Native American animal wisdom teaches us that each animal has a purpose, a gift to offer us. Seeing a specific animal is important because it carries within it a type of spiritual "medicine." For example, a wolf signifies "teacher," and if one encounters a wolf, whether an actual sighting of a wolf or in a dream, it signals that teaching in some way is very important. It may be that learning from or teaching another person is about to happen or needs to happen. It could also mean that a big life lesson of some kind is on the way, that life is about to teach something in particular.

Or, if one sees a fox trotting across a field or road, another kind of message is delivered. A fox symbolizes "becoming invisible," and a person may need to try to be less obvious and to enter places more quietly, without being noticed. Rabbits, dogs, birds, and all living creatures carry for us specific messages, and when we pay attention to that, it makes for a much more wondrously fulfilling day. Watch for animals you may see as you do what must be done, and make note of them, and look up the symbolic meaning of the animal. Ponder your own memories or associations with that particular kind of animal, and allow the wisdom that it offers to benefit you.

MY OWL MEDICINE MESSAGE

I hear an owl often, day or night. In my middle-school years I chose owl as my favorite bird and began collecting owl figures. I perceived them as wise, with their extraordinary vision abilities, and their mysteriousness had me spellbound. Through the years I learned that Apache tribal members do not see the owl as a good sign, but rather as a bad omen. One Apache friend was very upset about a white owl feather I had on my bookshelf. I didn't exactly share the Apache view of the meaning of owl, but began to understand that if I hear an owl, I need to pay attention and be ready for possible events that may impact me or many. At one point I recall someone offering me a small owl sculpture and I almost hesitated to accept it. But I did and thanked the person who gave me the owl sculpture because I realized that there was something coming and I needed to be alert. That turned out to be true, and it was a challenging time that followed, but I was grateful for the synchronistic convergence of being offered an owl figure and then facing an impending difficulty because I felt the owl message had tipped me off. I was able to have more courage, I think, because I was aware that something was up, and therefore more ready to handle it.

TRICKSTER MEDICINE

Another animal that carried a fairy message for me was the coyote. It was an eerie night when an entire pack of coyotes gathered, howling, under my bedroom window. They were so close I could hear them salivating. They howled and circled; their pack seemed to be in a frenzy just outside, under an almost full moon. I remember saying out loud, "Uh-oh. This is trouble. This means something is up and I don't like it!" Coyote medicine is that of the trickster, and there is some crazy trouble when you have a pack of them howling and spitting just under your window. And that turned out to be true! There was deception and trickery of many kinds that had a major impact on my life. I didn't like the feeling of trouble and dread that came with the unusual coyote visit but I was grateful for the spiritual support I received and knew that the fairies worked through the coyotes to keep me safe by alerting me.

Fairies are part of this body of knowledge known as animal wisdom and the Native American tribes knew that rather than being separate from animals, we are deeply entwined with them in spiritual ways. When Europeans swept through taking over the land the tribes inhabited, there was no real sense of that strong, spiritual connection to the land and its animals by the advancing pioneers. The pioneers wanted to tame the land and bring their notion of civilization to it, but I believe that to be truly civilized we need to do as the Native Americans have done and that is to honor and respect the land and animals among us, and receive the messages that come to us from the animal world.

FAIRIES AND BIRDS

For centuries, many people have seen the appearance of birds as gifts and signs, such as the cardinal, the crow, and hawks or eagles. Common birds such as robins or wrens became bringers of news, so if someone overheard or learned of a secret, they might have said, "A little birdy told me" when asked to report how they found out.

"Red Jays" and Blue Jays

When I see cardinals, I know it is a "hello" from my maternal grandmother, who called them "red jays." I know my grandmother loves me and is working with the fairies and the birds to give me messages of love and care. Likewise, if I see feathers float from above to the ground, I see it as a sign from my mother as one appeared in this way only a few days after her funeral. And I often ask for signs from birds and other animals, and look for them to appear.

Angels and animal spirits or fairies work closely together to help us stay aligned with our souls and to help us in our day-to-day lives. No day has to be dull or ordinary. They can provide powerful synchronistic episodes and realizations that can be life changing. Fairies will come through animals to talk with us, warn us, guide us, and lead us to happiness.

INSECT FAIRIES AND THE BASIC ELEMENTS OF LIFE

The green bug sleeps in the white lily ear.
The red bug sleeps in the white magnolia.
Shiny wings, you are choosers of color.
You have taken your summer bungalows wisely.
—"SMALL HOMES," CARL SANDBURG

WE SHARE OUR OWN DWELLINGS, PLACES, and spaces with all kinds of insects. Usually at the sight of them, I cringe or quiver, unless it is a ladybug, which I find adorable, or a dragonfly, which we know is an iridescent little wizard coming to grace us. Or the praying mantis and all the butterflies—they're wonderful. But I still generally expect insects to keep away from me as they might be biters, which means I have not fostered an affinity with them. But that has changed.

What I've been shown about our spirit world and the life essence permeating matter has altered my perspective in unexpected ways. I was greatly surprised and I have had to get used to it.

One fairy vision I see regularly is that of luminescent orbs of light, which are the basic "new life forms" within our universe. This is pure, new soul energy. They are blissful to perceive. My Cherokee mentor, Karen Land "Four Stars," explained that these new vital spirits are "the babies" and they observe us as they, in their newness, have not yet incarnated as souls into physical form. They glide and bring with them a feeling of pure love. And what I've seen in some of the orbs seems to tell me about our basic created world.

I see that some of the orbs of shimmering, pearlescent pink light (blissful to behold) have what looks like a busy bee inside it—also made of the same shimmering beautiful light. But this insect spirit inside the pearlescent orb creates new small orbs that are then born out of the larger orb. I see the bee-like spirit working with its small bee forelegs, and a tiny ball of light forms, and then the ball of light is released as a new small orb, and glides away. This process continues over and over while I watch. It is fascinating, it is breathtaking. But I must admit that when I first saw this, I was shocked and resistant.

Even though the vision is full of love and such a heavenly feeling, I was stunned about the insect part of it—and said to myself with a feeling of sci-fi horror, "Oh no! When we all die, we have no idea, we will see that God is this *giant insect*!" The Great Creator, based on this vision, is a creating busy bee. How could that be?!

After thinking it through, I calmed down and considered that while humans love to imagine fairies and angels as cherubs or be-winged, gracious, idealistic humans. What we are truly made of is more insect-like than we'd like to acknowledge. In our daily comings and goings as we see our reflection in mirrors or windows, we pass by and see our clothes, our hair, and our overall surface appearance. Taking a look at us through a microscope though we have a lot of tiny particles like bacteria, and it does not resemble cherubs. It more so resembles strange plasmatic sea creatures. Atoms look like miniature galaxies and our cells, our DNA chromosomes, are very insect like—more than I'm comfortable admitting because of the aversion I have to insects. What I had to acknowledge when I first started seeing the orb and the bee, was that we are made up of basic elements of life and that nature creates itself into being—constantly.

Yes, there are "busy bees" moment by moment spinning new life out of pure light and the pure essence of life. Nature Fairies! When we see living creatures, including insects, in our environment, we can quietly know that they are regally alive in our world as components of our very own aliveness, if we did not know it already, and feel that deep affinity with them, right down to our deepest levels of being, our strangely insect-like microorganisms!

LET THE FAIRY ADVENTURES BEGIN!

We have always had fairies in our midst, and always will. Being open to their existence is life enhancing, allowing the very notion of fairies to give us a sense of wonderment is excellent for us as creators in our own right, masters of our own limitless potential through our imagination. Finding the fairy spirits nearest you will be easy once your heart is open to them, knowing they are wherever you are, and ever will be. For fairies do wander everywhere!

ABOUT THE AUTHOR

ELAINE CLAYTON is an author, artist, Reiki Master, and intuitive reader. She writes and illustrates books for children, including books by Pulitzer Prize–winning author Jane Smiley and by Gregory Maguire, author of *Wicked*, which was adapted into the popular Broadway musical of the same name. She has two sons, Jonah and Alistair, and lives in Connecticut. She is the author of *A Little Bit of Angels*.

INDEX